DET
DANSKE
INSTITUT
I ATHEN

ΙΝΣΤΙΤΟΥΤΟ ΤΗΣ ΔΑΝΙΑΣ ΣΤΗΝ ΑΘΗΝΑ

THE DANISH INSTITUTE AT ATHENS

# Videnskab & Kunst

# Science & Art

# Επιστήμη & Τέχνη

Erik Hallager

in collaboration with

Jesper Jensen, Søren Dietz (S.D.), Bjørn Lovén, Mette Schaldemose (M.S.), Niels Andreasen,
Lone Simone Simonsen & Birgitte Kofoed Fudas

and with catalogue descriptions by

Μαρία Ανδρεαδάκη–Βλαζάκη (Μ.Α.-V.), Μαρία Γιαννοπούλου (M.G.), Ιωάννης Μόσχος (I.M.),
Ευτυχία Πρωτοπαπαδάκη (E.P.), & Κατερίνα Τζανακάκη (K.T.)

© Copyright The Danish Institute at Athens, Athens 2006
Science & Art
- *present activities of the Danish Institute at Athens*


Editors: Birgitta P. Hallager and Erik Hallager
Graphic design: Erik Hallager
Printed at Karydakis Leonidas


The publication was sponsored by:
Ny Carlsbergfondet


ISBN: 87-7934-117-9

Distributed by:
AARHUS UNIVERSITY PRESS
Langelandsgade 177
DK-8200 Århus N
Fax (+45) 8942 5380

73 Lime Walk
Headington, Oxford OX3 7AD
Fax (+44) 865 750 079

Box 511
Oakvill, Conn. 06779
Fax (+1) 203 945 94 9468


Cover illustrations:
Front: From the Megaron Mousikis exhibition November 2005;
excavations in the courtyard building in Kalydon October 2005;
first volume of the Chalkis excavations; and Vini Iuel together with
Thomas Clausen and his Brazilian trio give a concert in the lecture
hall of the Danish Institute.
Back: The Danish Institute at Athens in the Ag. Aikaterini Square
in Plaka.
The photographs are from the archive of the Danish Institute.

# Indhold / Contents / Περιεχόμενα

# Forord / Preface / Πρόλογος

I anledning af Hendes Majestæt Dronning Margrethe IIs officielle besøg i Grækenland den 24.-25. maj 2006 har Det Danske Institut i Athen forberedt en udstilling om Instituttet og dets akademiske medarbejderes igangværende aktiviteter.

Udstillingen fortæller i mange billeder og få ord om disse aktiviteter. Instituttets videnskabelige og kulturelle virksomhed belyses desuden gennem udstillede genstande dels fra arkæologiske udgravninger, dels af kunstværker, der er fremstillet som et resultat af kunstneres ophold ved Det Danske Institut.

Denne lille bog er bygget op over udstillingens materiale og desuden forsynet med en indledning om danskere, der har arbejdet med græsk arkæologi, og hvis indsats er en del af forhistorien til Instituttets grundlæggelse i 1992.

At udstilling og bog er blevet en realitet skyldes en stor hjælp og goodwill fra mange hold. Instituttet skylder eforerne for de involverede eforater en varm tak for deres tilladelse til, at de arkæologiske genstande kunne udstilles: Dr. M. Stavropoulou-Gatsi fra Mesolongi, Dr. A. Delaporta fra undervandseforatet, Dr. E. Konsolaki fra eforatet i Piræus og Dr. M. Andreadaki-Vlazaki fra eforatet i Khania. Vi er det centrale arkæologiske råd (KAS) og det græske kulturministerium og direktøren for afdeling for museer og udstillinger, Dr. Maria Pandou

On the occasion of the official visit of Her Majesty the Queen Margrethe II to Greece on the 24th – 25th of May 2006, the Danish Institute at Athens has prepared an exhibition about the ongoing activities of the Institute and its academic staff.

Through many pictures and few words the exhibition describes these activities. Likewise the scientific and cultural work of the Institute are visualised through the exhibited items, partly from the archaeological excavations, partly from the works of art which are results of the artists' stay at the Danish Institute.

This book is based on the contents of the exhibition and includes a preface about the Danes who have worked with Greek archaeology and whose work partly was the preliminary to the foundation of the Institute in 1992.

The realization of the exhibition and this book is due to assistance and goodwill from many sides. The Institute owes a warm thank to the ephors at the involved ephorates for giving their permission to exhibit the archaeological items: Dr M. Stavropoulou-Gatsi from Mesolongi, Dr. A. Delaporta from the Underwater Ephorate, Dr. E. Konsolaki from the Ephorate in Pireus, and Dr. M. Andreadaki-Vlazaki from the Ephorat in Khania. We are deeply grateful to The Central Archaeological Board (KAS), The Greek Ministry of Cul-

Με την ευκαιρία της επίσιμης επίσκεψης της Α.Μ. Βασίλισσας Μαργρέτε Β΄ στην Ελλάδα στις 24-25 Μαΐου 2006, το Ινστιτούτο της Δανίας στην Αθήνα ετοίμασε μία έκθεση για το ίδιο και τις δραστηριότητές του.

Με πολλές φωτογραφίες και λίγες λέξεις η έκθεση αυτή περιγράφει τις δραστηριότητες του Ινστιτούτου, ενώ τα εκθέματα, αρχαιολογικά ευρήματα από τις ανασκαφές του και έργα που φιλοτεχνήθηκαν από καλλιτέχνες κατά την παραμονή τους σε αυτό, ζωντανεύουν το επιστημονικό και πολιτιστικό του έργο.

Το παρόν βιβλίο, το οποίο είναι βασισμένο στην έκθεση, περιλαμβάνει εισαγωγή για τους Δανούς αρχαιολόγους που εργάστηκαν στην Ελλάδα και των οποίων το έργο έθεσε εν πολλοίς τις βάσεις για την ίδρυση του Ινστιτούτου το 1992.

Τόσο η έκθεση όσο και το βιβλίο αυτό δεν θα μπορούσαν να πραγματοποιηθούν χωρίς τη συνδρομή πολυάριθμων προσώπων και φορέων. Για την άδεια παρουσίασης των εκθεμάτων, το Ινστιτούτο οφείλει κατ'αρχάς να ευχαριστήσει τους προϊσταμένους των εκάστοτε εφορείων αρχαιοτήτων και συγκεκριμένα τη Δρ. Μ. Σταυροπούλου-Γάτση της ΛΣΤ΄ Εφορείας Προϊστορικών και Κλασικών Αρχαιοτήτων, τη Δρ. Α. Δελαπόρτα της Εφορείας Εναλίων Αρχαιοτήτων, τη Δρ. Ε. Κονσολάκη της ΚΣΤ΄ ΕΠΚΑ και τη Δρ. Μ. Ανδρεαδάκη-Βλαζάκη της

dybt taknemmelige for det gode samarbejde og de ministerielle og endelige tilladelser.

Instituttet ønsker desuden at takke de forskellige projekters ledere og medhjælpere for det store arbejde de har lagt i at finde billeder og fremstille tekster til udstilling og bog. Vi er ligeledes de involverede kunstnere taknemmelige for den ildhu, med hvilken de er gået aktivt ind i projektet.

Personligt vil jeg bringe en varm tak til Hanna Lassen og Instituttets øvrige stab og venner for den uvurderlige arbejdsindsats, de har ydet. Af disse rettes en speciel tak til Jesper Jensen og Michalis Lefantzis, der har lay-outet alle udstillingens 15 plancher. Ligeledes en varm til Birgitta P. Hallager, der har redigeret denne bog – og til alle andre, der også har hjulpet os.

Vi er Stuart Heath taknemmelig for at have korrigeret de engelske tekster og dr. Maria Xanthopoulou for oversættelserne til græsk.

Sidst men ikke mindst ønsker jeg at udtrykke min taknemmelighed til de institutioner og fonde hvis økonomiske støtte har gjort udstillingen mulig: Kunststyrelsen i det danske Kulturministerium og Ny Carlsbergfondet, der har bekostet trykning af bogen.

Athen, den 8. maj 2006
Erik Hallager

ture, and the Director of the Department of Museums and Exhibitions Dr. Maria Pandou for good cooperation and the final permissions.

Besides, the Institute wishes to thank the directors and their assistants of all the projects for their industrious work with selecting pictures and producing texts for the exhibition and the book. Furthermore, we are grateful to the involved artists for their enthusiastic work with this project.

Personally, I would like to warmly thank Ms Hanna Lassen and other employees and friends of the Institute for their invaluable contribution of work. Among these a special thank goes to Jesper Jensen and Dr. Michalis Lefantzis who have lay-outed all 15 posters. Besides, a warm thank to Birgitta P. Hallager who edited this book – and to everybody else who have helped us.

We are grateful to Stuart Heath for proof-reading the English texts and to Dr. Maria Xanthopoulou for the translation into Greek.

Last but not least, I wish to express my gratitude towards the institutions and foundations whose economic support has made this exhibition possible: The Danish Arts Agency of the Ministry of Culture, and The New Carlsberg Foundation who have defrayed the expenses of printing the book.

Athens, 8 May 2006.
Erik Hallager

ΚΕ΄ ΕΠΚΑ. Ευχαριστούμε επίσης το Κεντρικό Αρχαιολογικό Συμβούλιο, το Υπουργείο Πολιτισμού, και την προϊσταμένη της Διεύθυνσης Μουσείων και Εκθέσεων, Δρ. Μαρία Πάντου, για την καλή συνεργασία και τις τελικές άδειες.

Θερμές ευχαριστίες οφείλουμε επίσης στους διευθυντές και συνεργάτες όλων των προγραμμάτων του Ινστιτούτου για την επιλογή των φωτογραφιών και τη συγγραφή των κειμένων της έκθεσης και του βιβλίου, όπως και στους καλλιτέχνες που συνεργάστηκαν με ενθουσιασμό για την πραγματοποίηση αυτής της εκδήλωσης.

Προσωπικά επιθυμώ να ευχαριστήσω την κυρία Hanna Lassen και τους άλλους υπαλλήλους και φίλους του Ινστιτούτου για την πολύτιμη συνεργασία τους. Τους κυρίους Jesper Jensen και Μιχάλη Λεφαντζή ευχαριστώ ιδιαίτερα για τη στοιχειοθεσία των πόστερ. Ευχαριστώ επίσης θερμά την Birgitta P. Hallager για την επιμέλεια του βιβλίου, τον κ. Stuart Heath για την επιμέλεια του αγγλικού κειμένου, τη Δρ. Μαρία Ξανθοπούλου για την ελληνική μετάφραση και όλους όσους μας βοήθησαν.

Τέλος, θα ήθελα να ευχαριστήσω τους φορείς και τα ιδρύματα που με τη χρηματοδότησή τους κατέστησαν δυνατή την υλοποίηση της έκθεσης και του παρόντος βιβλίου, και συγκεκριμένα τη Διεύθυνση Τεχνών του Υπουργείου Πολιτισμού της Δανίας, και το ίδρυμα Ny Carlsbergfondet.

Αθήνα, 8 Μαΐου 2006
Erik Hallager

# Danskere i græsk arkæologi
# Danes in Greek archaeology
# Οι Δανοί στην ελληνική αρχαιολογία

Dansk engagement i græsk arkæologi går helt tilbage til Tyrkertiden. I det sene 1700- og tidlige 1800-tal var det kommet på mode blandt europæiske intellektuelle at studere den græske fortid. Det gjaldt også Peter Oluf Brønsted, der var en fremtrædende klassisk filolog og arkæolog. I perioden 1810-13 rejste han rundt i Syditalien, Lilleasien og Grækenland, hvor han mødte filhellenere som K. Haller von Hallerstein, J. Linchk, O. von Stackelberg, R. Cockerell og J. Foster. I vinteren 1811-12 foretog Brøndsted udgravninger på øen Kea.

Resultaterne af hans undersøgelser på Kea, der indeholdt en beskrivelse af de antikke byer, deres geografi og historie samt historiske monumenter med speciel vægt lagt på udgravningerne af Karthaia, blev publiceret i første bind af hans hovedværk *Voyages dans la Grèce accompagnés de recherches archaeologiques, I-II. Paris 1826-30.* Bogen, der blev trykt på såvel fransk som tysk, gav ham international anerkendelse.

Senere i 1812 arbejdede Brønsted sammen med Cockerell, Foster, von Hallerstein og Linckh på deres udgravninger af templet i Bassai og hans notater fra udgravningerne

The Danish involvement in Greek archaeology goes back to the period of "Turkokratia". During the late 18th and early 19th centuries it had become fashionable among many European intellectuals to study the Greek past. This was true of Peter Oluf Brønsted, a very talented classical philologist and archaeologist. Between 1810-13 he travelled in Southern Italy, Asia Minor and Greece where he met philhellenics like von Hallerstein, Linckh, von Stackelberg, Cockerell and Foster. During the winter of 1811-12 Brønsted undertook excavations on the island of Kea.

The results of his investigations in Kea, which contained a description of the ancient cities, their geography, history and historical monuments with emphasis on his excavations of Karthaia were published in the first volume of his major work "Voyages dans la Grèce accompagnés de recherches archaeologiques, I-II. Paris 1826-30. The book was printed both in French and German and brought him international recognition.

Later in 1812 Brønsted joined Cockerell, Foster, von Hallerstein and Linckh in their excavations of the temple at Bassai and his notes became an important and integral

Η ενασχόληση των Δανών με την ελληνική αρχαιολογία ξεκίνησε ήδη από τα χρόνια της Τουρκοκρατίας, καθώς η μελέτη του ελληνικού παρελθόντος ήταν προσφιλής στους ευρωπαίους διανοούμενους στα τέλη του 18ου αιώνα και στις αρχές του 19ου. Ο Δανός Peter Oluf Brønsted, ταλαντούχος φιλόλογος και αρχαιολόγος, ταξίδεψε το 1810-13 στην Νότια Ιταλία, τη Μικρά Ασία και την Ελλάδα, όπου συνάντησε τους φιλέλληνες Karl Haller von Hallerstein, J. Linckh, O. von Stackelberg, C. Robert Cockerell και J. Foster. Το χειμώνα του 1811-12, ο Brønsted πραγματοποίησε ανασκαφές στην Κέα.

Τα αποτελέσματα των ερευνών του στο νησί αυτό (ιστορία και γεωγραφία των αρχαίων πόλεων, περιγραφή αυτών και των κυριοτέρων μνημείων τους) δημοσιεύτηκαν στον πρώτο τόμο του σημαντικού έργου του *Voyages dans la Grèce accompagnés de recherches archéologiques*, I-II (Παρίσι), το οποίο κυκλοφόρησε στη γαλλική και γερμανική γλώσσα και του απέφερε διεθνή φήμη.

Το 1812 ο Brønsted συμμετείχε μαζί με τους Cockerell, Foster, von Hallerstein και Linckh στις ανασκαφές του ναού του Απόλλωνα στις Βάσσες και οι σημειώσεις τους βοήθησαν σημαντικά στη σύνταξη

P.O. Brønsted (1780-1842). Oil painting by C.A. Jensen.

Christian Hansen, Athens: The re-erection of the temple of Athena Nike 1836.

blev en meget vigtig del af publikationen, der udkom i 1860.

Efter frihedskrigen blev Athen Grækenlands hovedstad i 1834. I den forbindelse kom mange fremmede til byen for at hjælpe med at etablere den nye stat og planlægge og bygge den nye hovedstad. En af dem var den danske arkitekt Christian Hansen, som er bedst kendt for opførelsen af Athens Universitet. Han ankom til Athen i 1833, og allerede samme år havde han gjort mange tegninger og opmålinger af antikke monumenter. I samarbejde med professor Ross arbejdede Christian Hansen i 1830'erne med restaureringen af Athens Akropolis. En vigtig del af hans arbejde var at producere detaljerede tegninger af arkitekturfragmenter og keramik.

part of the final publication which appeared in 1860.

After the war of independence, in 1834 Athens became the capital of Greece. Many foreigners then came to Athens to help establishing the new state and to plan and build the new capital. One of them was Christian Hansen, the Danish architect who is best known for the University of Athens. He arrived in Athens in 1833 and by the end of that year he had completed many drawings and taken measurements of the ancient monuments. During the 1830s, in collaboration with Professor Ross, Christian Hansen worked on the restoration of the Athenian Acropolis. An important part of his work consisted of the detailed drawings of finds such as architectural members and pottery.

της τελικής δημοσίευσης της ανασκαφής το 1860.

Μετά το πέρας της ελληνικής επανάστασης και την εκλογή της Αθήνας ως πρωτεύουσας το 1834, πολλοί ξένοι μετέβησαν στην Αθήνα για να βοηθήσουν στη λειτουργία του νεοσύστατου κράτους και στην ανοικοδόμηση της νέας του πρωτεύουσας. Ο Δανός αρχιτέκτονας Christian Hansen, ευρύτερα γνωστός για το κτίριο του Πανεπιστημίου της Αθήνας, έφτασε στη Αθήνα το 1833 και μέχρι το τέλος του ίδιου χρόνου πραγματοποίησε πλήθος σχεδίων και μετρήσεων των αρχαίων μνημείων της πόλης. Τη δεκαετία του 1830, σε συνεργασία με τον καθηγητή Ross, ο Hansen εργάστηκε για την αναστήλωση της Ακρόπολης. Σημαντικό μέρος της δουλειάς του αποτέλεσε η λεπτομερής σχεδιαστική αποτύπωση

Christian Hansen, Capital, Acropolis Athens, May 1836.

Hansen's drawing of the griffin vase, 1837.

Hans Christian Andersen's version of the same vase, March 1841.

En af disse var grifvasen, som Hansen tegnede på Ægina i 1837, og som senere blev opbevaret i et magasin på Akropolis. I 1841 besøgte vores store eventyrdigter H.C. Andersen Akropolis gentagne gange, og han blev så fascineret af vasen, at han lavede en skitse af den i sin dagbog - en af de meget få skitser fra hans rejse til Grækenland.

I slutningen af 1800-tallet påbegyndte mange lande storstilede arkæologiske ekspeditioner i Grækenland, og på et vist tidspunkt ville Danmark også følge trop. Initiativet hertil kom fra den klassiske filolog og arkæolog Karl Frederik Kinck, der - med Carlsbergfondets accept - foreslog øen Rhodos som et passende sted for omfattende arkæologiske undersøgelser. Samtidigt blev den dygtige og erfarne udgraver Christian Blinkenberg udnævnt til at

The griffin vase was drawn by Hansen on Aigina in 1837, it was later kept in a storeroom at the Acropolis. In 1841 our great storyteller Hans Christian Andersen visited the Acropolis several times and he became so fascinated by the vase that he made a sketch of it in his diary – one of the few sketches he made during his visit to Greece.

In the later part of the 19th century many countries began large-scale archaeological expeditions within Greece. Also Denmark wanted to follow suit. Karl Frederik Kinck a classical philologist and archaeologist took the initiative and the Carlsberg Foundation accepted the proposal of Rhodes as a suitable place for large archaeological investigations. At the time Christian Blinkenberg, an experienced field archaeologist, was appointed to

αρχαιολογικών ευρημάτων, όπως αρχιτεκτονικών μελών και κεραμικής.

Το αγγείο με τους γρύπες που ο Hansen σχεδίασε στην Αίγινα το 1837 και που έπειτα μεταφέρθηκε στις αποθήκες της Ακρόπολης, είδε και ο διάσημος Δανός παραμυθάς Hans Christian Andersen, σε μια από τις πολλές επισκέψεις του στο μνημείο. Ο Andersen εντυπωσιάστηκε τόσο ώστε αποθανάτισε το αγγείο στο ημερολόγιό του, σ' ένα από τα ελάχιστα σκαριφίματα που φιλοτέχνησε κατά τη διαμονή του στην Ελλάδα.

Τον ύστερο 19ο αιώνα, αρκετές χώρες ξεκίνησαν εκτεταμένες αρχαιολογικές έρευνες στην Ελλάδα. Η Δανία ακολούθησε το ρεύμα της εποχής. Με πρωτοβουλία του Karl Frederick Kinck, κλασικού φιλολόγου και αρχαιολόγου, επιλέχθηκε η Ρόδος ως ο καταλληλότερος τόπος για τη διενέργεια ανασκαφών. Το

17

Ejnar Dyggve's reconstruction of the temple of Athena on the Acropolis of Lindos.

Excavators and visitors at the Acropolis of Lindos in March 1903. Blinkenberg with a stick sits in the foreground while Kinck stands in the centre. To the left of Kinck is Ms. Hedvig Amsinck later to become Mrs. Kinck.

forestå udgravningerne sammen med Kinck.

Ekspeditionen arbejdede fra 1902 til 1914, og udgravninger og opmålninger af synlige antikke monumenter foregik over hele den sydlige del af øen. I Vati området udgravede Kinck mykenske kammergrave, i Exochi grave fra geometrisk tid, mens han i Vroulia udgravede store dele af en arkaiske garnisionsby.

Ekspeditionens vigtigste resultat var imidlertid udgravningen af Lindos' akropol med Athenetemplet. Det tog 90 år at publicere ekspeditionen. Det sidste bind udkom i 1992.

conduct the excavations alongside Kinck.

The expedition lasted from 1902 to 1914 during which time excavations and measurements of visible remains from antiquity took place across the southern part of the island. Kinck excavated Mycenaean chamber tombs at Vati, Geometric tombs at Exochi, while the archaic settlement at Vroulia was partly excavated.

The major achievement of the expedition, however, was the excavation of the Acropolis of Lindos with the temple of Athena. It took 90 years to finish the publication of the expedition.

Ίδρυμα Carlsberg ανέλαβε τη χρηματοδότηση και ο έμπειρος αρχαιολόγος Christian Blinkenberg κλήθηκε να διευθύνει τις ανασκαφές μαζί με τον Kinck.

Οι έρευνες, οι οποίες διήρκεσαν από το 1902 ως το 1914, περιλάμβαναν ανασκαφές και καταγραφή των ορατών αρχαιολογικών λειψάνων στο νότιο τμήμα του νησιού. Ο Kinck ανέσκαψε θαλαμωτούς τάφους της Μυκηναϊκής εποχής στο Βάτι και τάφους της Γεωμετρικής εποχής στη θέση Εξοχή, ενώ ανέσκαψε μερικώς τον αρχαϊκό οικισμό στη Βρουλιά.

Το σημαντικότερο όμως επίτευγμα της αποστολής ήταν η ανασκαφή της ακρόπολης της Λίνδου και του εκεί ναού της Αθηνάς, η δημοσίευση της οποίας χρειάστηκε ενενήντα χρόνια για να ολοκληρωθεί.

Halvor Bagge's colour drawing of a Marine Style stirrup jar from Gournia.

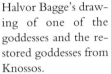

Halvor Bagge's drawing of one of the goddesses and the restored goddesses from Knossos.

Mens Blinkenberg og Kinck udgravede på Rhodos, arbejdede den ganske ukendte danske kunstner, Halvor Bagge, på Peloponnes og på Kreta. Vi ved fra Sir Arthur Evans' regnskaber, at han var på Knossos i flere sæsoner. De mest berømte fund han restaurerede, var de såkaldte slangegudinder fra skatkamret i paladsets vestfløj. Da han arbejdede med figurerne, opdagede han, at en lille løvinde passede til en hovedbeklædning, og at begge med største sandsynlighed hørte til den dårligst bevarede af de to fajancefigurer. Som Evans skrev i første bind af sin Knossos publikation: "Denne iagttagelseblev først gjort af kunstneren Hr. Halvor Bagge...".

Af andre varige arbejder fra Bagges hånd kan nævnes de fremragende farve- og samleplancher, i Harriet Boyds publikation af Gournia fra 1908.

At the time when Blinkenberg and Kinck worked on Rhodes, an unknown Danish artist, Halvor Bagge, worked in the Peleponnese and in Crete. We know from Sir Arthur Evans' accounts that he was, for several seasons, at Knossos. The most well known pieces he restored, were the Snake-goddesses from the Temple Repositories. While he worked with the two figures, he discovered that a miniature lioness fitted to a headpiece and that they both almost certainly belonged to the least well preserved of the two figures. As Evans writes in the first volume of his Knossos publication "This observation was first made by the artist Mr. Halvor Bagge...".

Other lasting works from Bagge include the excellent colour and collective plates found in Harriet Boyd's publication of Gournia from 1908.

Όσο οι Blinkenberg και Kinck εργάζονταν στη Ρόδο, ένας άγνωστος καλλιτέχνης, ο Δανός Halvor Bagge, γύριζε την Πελοπόννησο και την Κρήτη. Γνωρίζουμε από αναφορές του Arthur Evans ότι ο Bagge εργάστηκε επί σειρά ετών στην Κνωσό, όπου συντήρησε μεταξύ άλλων αρχαιοτήτων και τις Θεές των Όφεων από τους Θησαυρούς του Ιερού. Μάλιστα, στον πρώτο τόμο της δημοσίευσης της ανασκαφής του ανακτόρου ο Evans αναφέρει ότι "πρώτος ο καλλιτέχνης κύριος Halvor Bagge παρατήρησε" πως μικρογραφική λέαινα ανήκε σε διάδημα το οποίο ανήκε με τη σειρά του στο λιγότερο καλά διατηρημένο αγαλματίδιο.

Έργα του Bagge είναι άλλωστε και οι θαυμάσιες υδατογραφίες, αλλά και οι συνοπτικοί πίνακες, που δημοσιεύτηκαν από τη Harriet Boyd στην έκθεση της ανασκαφής Γουρνιών το 1908.

The Heroon at Kalydon was excavated during the years 1926, 1928 and 1932.

I tiden mellem de to Verdenskrige var det stadig muligt at foretage udgravninger i Grækenland, uden at man havde et arkæologisk institut. Således tog den græske arkæolog Konstantinos Rhomaios og den danske arkæolog og filhellen Fredrik Poulsen i 1920'erne initiativ til at begynde udgravninger i den antikke by Kalydon i Vestgrækenland. Fredrik Poulsen havde i sin ungdom rejst over det meste af Grækenland, og da udgravningerne startede, var han direktør for Ny Carlsberg Glyptotek. Poulsen deltog selv i udgravningerne i 1926, 1928 og 1932,

In the time between the two World Wars it was still possible to organise excavations in Greece without having a school. In the 1920s Konstantinos Rhomaios, the Greek archaeologist and Frederik Poulsen the Danish archaeologist and philhellene took the initiative and started excavations in ancient city of Kalydon in western Greece. In his youth Frederik Poulsen had travelled over most of Greece and the start of the excavation he was Director of the Ny Carlsberg Glyptotek. Poulsen participated in the excavations in 1926, 1928 and 1932.

Στο Μεσοπόλεμο ήταν ακόμη δυνατή η διεξαγωγή ανασκαφών από ξένους αρχαιολόγους, τον οποίων η χώρα δεν διέθετε μόνιμη αρχαιολογική αποστολή, ή Σχολή, στην Ελλάδα. Τη δεκαετία του 1920, ο Έλληνας αρχαιολόγος Κωνσταντίνος Ρωμαίος και ο Δανός αρχαιολόγος και φιλέλληνας Frederik Poulsen ξεκίνησαν ανασκαφές στην αρχαία Καλυδώνα Αιτωλίας. Ως νέος αρχαιολόγος ο Poulsen είχε περιηγηθεί ολόκληρη σχεδόν την Ελλάδα και όταν ξεκίνησαν οι έρευνες στην Καλυδώνα κατείχε τη θέση του διευθυντή του μουσείου Ny Carlsberg

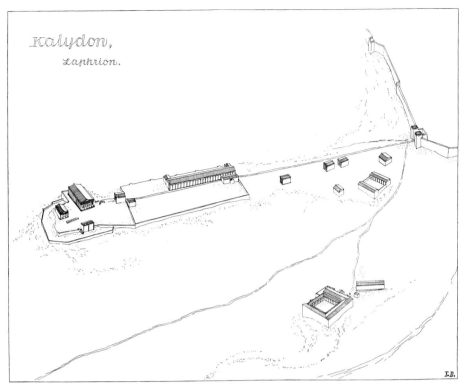

Fredrik Poulsen (1876-1950).

Ejnar Dyggve (1887-1961).

Ejnar Dygge's isometric reconstruction of the Temple area at Kalydon from his 1948 publication.

mens de sidste to kampagner i 1935 og 1938 blev gennemført under ledelse af af den danske arkitekt og arkæolog Ejnar Dyggve.

Ejnar Dyggve, der var uddannet på Det Kongelige Danske Kunstakademi i København, er bedst kendt for sine omfattende udgravninger af den tidligkristne by i Salona i Serbien. Han arbejdede i adskillige år med Kalydon-materialet. De vigtigste bygninger, der blev udgravet, var templet til Artemis Lauphria og det såkaldte Heroon, og Dyggve var ansvarlig for størstedelen af den endelige publikation af udgravningerne.

The last two campaigns carried out in 1935 and 1938 were conducted by the Danish architect and archaeologist Ejnar Dyggve.

Ejnar Dyggve, who was educated at the Royal Danish Academy of Fine Arts in Copenhagen, is best known for his large scale excavations of the early Christian settlement at Salona in Serbia. He worked for several years with the Kalydon material. The major buildings excavated included the Temple of Artemis Lauphria and the so called Heroon. Dyggve was responsible for the majority of the publication of the excavations.

Glyptotek. Ο Poulsen συμμετείχε στις ανασκαφές του 1926, 1928 και 1932. Τις δύο τελευταίες αποστολές στην Καλυδώνα (1935 και 1938) διήυθηνε ο Δανός αρχιτέκτονας και αρχαιολόγος Ejnar Dyggve. Απόφοιτος της Ακαδημίας Καλών Τεχνών της Κοπεγχάγης, ο Dyggve έγινε ευρύτερα γνωστός για τις ανασκαφές του στην παλαιοχριστιανική πόλη των Σαλόνων στη Σερβία. Μελέτησε για πολλά χρόνια το υλικό από τις ανασκαφές της Καλυδώνας, ανέσκαψε το ναό τις Λαφρίας Αρτέμιδος και το λεγόμενο Ηρώο και ήταν υπεύθυνος για τις περισσότερες δημοσιεύσεις της ανασκαφής.

Erik Hansen at Delphi.

Erik Hansen's reconstruction of the Treasury of the Siphnians from the 1987 publication.

I Danmark siges det, at alle arkitekter af betydning på et eller andet tidspunkt i deres liv har arbejdet for Den Franske Skole i Athen. Eksempelvis kan nævnes Vilhelm Lauritsen, Kaj Gottlob og Gregers Algreen-Ussing. Erik Hansen er dog den mest berømte i arkæologiske kredse. Han har i mere end 45 år arbejdet i Delfi, hvor han har været ansvarlig for de detaljerede planer over helligdommen, ligesom han har publiceret Sifniernes skatkammer og for ganske nylig afleveret det endelige manuskript vedrørende Apollon-templet.

Efter 2. Verdenskrig var det ikke længere muligt for udlændinge at foretage udgravninger i Grækenland uden at have et arkæologisk institut, men danske arkæologer var alligevel med takket være Det Svenske

There is a saying in Denmark that all architects of importance at some point in their life have worked for the French School at Athens; for example, Vilhelm Lauritsen, Kaj Gottlob and Gregers Algreen-Ussing, while in archaeological circles the most famous is Erik Hansen. He has worked for more than 45 years at Delphi where he has been responsible for the detailed plans of the sanctuary. Furthermore he has published the treasury of the Siphnians and recently he has also delivered the final manuscript on the temple of Apollo.

After the Second World War it was no longer possible for foreign archaeologists to excavate in Greece without an archaeological institute, but Danish archaeologists were at work thanks to the Swedish Insti-

Στη Δανία λένε ότι όλοι οι σημαντικοί αρχιτέκτονες συνεργάστηκαν σε κάποια στιγμή της ζωής τους με τη Γαλλική Σχολή Αθηνών. Τη ρήση αυτή επιβεβαιώνουν οι Vilhelm Lauritsen, Kaj Gottlob και Gregers Algreen-Ussing, αλλά και ο πιο γνωστός στους αρχαιολογικούς κύκλους Erik Hansen, ο οποίος εργάστηκε στις ανασκαφές των Δελφών για περισσότερα από 45 χρόνια ως υπεύθυνος για τη λεπτομερή αποτύπωση του ιερού. Ο Hansen δημοσίευσε επίσης το Θησαυρό των Σιφνίων, ενώ πρόσφατα παρέδωσε το χειρόγραφο για τη δημοσίευση του ναού του Απόλλωνα.

Μετά το Δεύτερο Παγκόσμιο Πόλεμο, η διενέργεια ανασκαφών από ξένους αρχαιολόγους ήταν δυνατή μόνο από μόνιμη αρχαιολογική αποστολή της χώρας τους στην Ελλάδα. Δανοί αρχαιολόγοι εργάστηκαν για μεγάλο

Publications by the Swedish Institute as a result of Danish involvement. To the left *Asine* II edited by Søren Dietz and to the right *The Greek Swedish Excavations* III.1 edited by Erik & Birgitta P. Hallager.

Institut i Athen. Vi er vort broderfolk taknemmelige, for deres generøse tilbud om at inkludere danske arkæologer i deres projekter. Således deltog et hold i 1971-74 i udgravningerne i Asine øst for akropolen og resultaterne herfra blev publiceret af Dr. Søren Dietz i 1982.

I 1971 blev Erik Hallager inviteret til at deltage i de græsk-svenske udgravninger i Khania Udgravningerne var startet to år tidligere under ledelse af Dr. Yannis Tzedakis daværende direktør for eforatet i Khania og professor Carl-Gustaf Styrenius, daværende direktør for det Svenske Institut i Athen. De første tre bind af udgravningerne udkom i 1997, 2000 og 2003.

I 1980'erne arbejdede interesserede parter hårdt på at få oprettet et dansk institut i Athen. Der var lange og vanskelige forhandlinger, men endelig gav den daværende undervisningsminister, Bertel Haarder, grønt lys, og Det Danske Institut blev indviet den 2. april 1992 med

tute at Athens. We are most grateful for their generous offer to include Danish archaeologists in their projects. As a result one team participated in 1971-74 in the Asine excavations east of the Acropolis, the results of which were published by Dr. Søren Dietz in 1982.

In 1971 Erik Hallager was invited to participate in the Greek-Swedish Excavations at Khania. The excavations had started two years earlier under direction of Dr. Yannis Tzedakis then director of the ephorate of Western Crete and Professor Carl-Gustaf Styrenius then Director of the Swedish Institute at Athens. The first three volumes of the excavations were published in 1997, 2000 and 2003.

During the 1980s interested parties in Denmark worked very hard in an attempt to establish an Institute in Athens. There were long and difficult negotiations but finally the then Minister of Education, Mr. Bertel Haarder, gave the "green light" and the Danish Institute was inaugurated

χρονικό διάστημα υπό την αιγίδα του Σουηδικού Ινστιτούτου Αθηνών, στο οποίο οφείλουμε θερμές ευχαριστίες για την προθυμία με την οποία συμπεριέλαβε Δανούς αρχαιολόγους στα προγράμματά του. Έτσι Δανοί αρχαιολόγοι εργάστηκαν στην Ασίνη, την περίοδο 1971-74, και τα αποτελέσματα των ερευνών τους δημοσιεύτηκαν από το Δρ. S. Dietz το 1982.

Ο Erik Hallager κλήθηκε το 1971 να συμμετάσχει στις ελληνο-σουηδικές ανασκαφές στα Χανιά, οι οποίες είχαν ξεκινήσει δύο χρόνια νωρίτερα υπό τη διεύθυνση του Δρ. Γ. Τζεδάκη, τότε προϊσταμένου της Εφορείας Π.Κ. Αρχαιοτήτων Δυτικής Κρήτης, και του καθηγητή C.-G. Styrenius, τότε διευθυντή του Σουηδικού Ινστιτούτου Αθηνών. Οι τρεις πρώτοι τόμοι της ανασκαφικής έκθεσης εκδόθηκαν το 1997-2003.

Κατά τη δεκαετία 1980, Δανοί ενδιαφερόμενοι εργάστηκαν σκληρά προκειμένου η χώρα τους να αποκτήσει τη δική της σχολή στην Ελλάδα. Έπειτα από διαβουλεύσεις, ο υπουργός παιδείας της Δανίας ο.κ. Bertel

The Danish Institute at Athens was inaugurated on the 2nd of April 1992 in four rooms rented from the student hostel at the Norwegian Institute, situated in Kavalotti Street next to the Nordic Library, shown is here under restoration.

Dr. Søren Dietz som dets første direktør. Med denne begivenhed fik Danmark også mulighed for at drive selvstændig arkæologisk forskning i Grækenland, ligesom andre fag, der arbejder med græsk historie, sprog og kultur, har fået en videnskabelig basis for at arbejde "i marken". Dette har været muligt takket være den generøse støtte, vi gennem alle årene har modtaget fra såvel det græske kulturministerium som de lokale arkæologiske myndigheder og institutioner, vi har samarbejdet med.

on the 2nd of April 1992 with Dr. Søren Dietz as the first Director. Since then the Danes have been able to conduct archaeological research within Greece and other disciplines that work with Greek history, language and culture have got a scientific basis for "field research". This was possible thanks to the generous support we have received throughout the years from the Greek Ministry of Culture and from the local archaeological ephorates and institutions with whom we have collaborated.

Haarder έδωσε το πράσινο φως και το Ινστιτούτο της Δανίας στην Αθήνα εγκαινιάστηκε στις 2 Απριλίου 1992 με πρώτο διευθυντή το Δρ. Søren Dietz. Έκτοτε το Ινστιτούτο της Δανίας προωθεί δικά του προγράμματα αρχαιολογικής έρευνας, ενώ και άλλοι επιστημονικοί κλάδοι που σχετίζονται με την ιστορία, τη γλώσσα και τον πολιτισμό της Ελλάδας βρήκαν στο Ινστιτούτο μια βάση για τη διενέργεια έρευνας πεδίου, πάντα με την υποστήριξη του ελληνικού Υπουργείου Πολιτισμού και των εκάστοτε τοπικών εφορειών αρχαιοτήτων και άλλων φορέων.

# Instituttet / The Institute / Το Ινστιτούτο

Efter den beskedne start i Kavalotti-gaden flyttede Instituttet i 1993 til dets nuværende lokaler i Herefondos 14 ved Ag. Aikaterini-pladsen i Plaka. Dette var muligt takket være en storslået donation fra Carlsbergfondet. Det unge Institut ville også meget gerne være i stand til at huse besøgende forskere og kunstnere, og da det lyseblå nabo-hus blev til salg, blev også dette

After the modest start in Kavalotti Street the Institute moved in 1993 to its present location in Herefondos 14, Ag. Aikaterini Square, Plaka. This was made possible through a grandiose donation from the Carlsberg Foundation. One of the wishes of the young Institute was to be able to accommodate visiting scholars and artists, so when the neighbouring, light blue building

Το Ινστιτούτο εγκαταστάθηκε αρχι-κά στην οδό Καβαλλότι, όμως το 1993, χάρη σε σημαντική δωρεά του Ιδρύματος Carlsberg, μεταφέρθηκε σε νεοκλασικό κτίριο στην οδό Χαι-ρεφώντος 14, στην πλατεία Αγίας Αικατερίνης στην Πλάκα. Με νέα δωρεά του Ιδρύματος Carlsberg αγο-ράστηκε και το διπλανό κτίριο, προκειμένου να μπορεί το Ινστι-τούτο να προσφέρει στέγη σε

17

doneret af Carlsbergfondet. Det indeholder nu tre lejligheder med fælles faciliteter som køkken, opholdsstue og internetadgang. En anden ting, der stod højt på Instituttets ønskeseddel, var et auditorium og mere kontorplads - og igen var vi heldige. Ved siden af Instituttet var der en ubebygget grund, og denne blev sammen med bygningen af et auditorium og tre kontorer skænket af Velux Fonden. Auditoriet, der blev indviet i 2000, har været centrum for det meste af Instituttets udadrettede virksomhed. Ud over disse bygninger lejer Instituttet en fireværelses lejlighed, der anvendes som studenterhybel, i den nærliggende Parthenonos gade.

came up for sale this was also donated by the Carlsberg Foundation. It now contains three flats with common amenities such as kitchen, living room and admission to internet. A further wish of the Institute was a lecture hall and more offices, and again we were lucky. Just next to the Institute was a vacant plot. This plot together with a lecture hall and offices above were donated by the Velux Foundation and inaugurated in year 2000. This hall has been the focal point for the major part of the public events held by the Institute. The Institute also rents a four-room flat in the nearby Parthenonos Street and used as a student hostel.

Δανούς ερευνητές και καλλιτέχνες που φιλοξενήθηκαν σε αυτό. Το κτίριο αυτό διαμορφώθηκε σε τρία διαμερίσματα με κοινόχρηστους βοηθητικούς χώρους. Οι ανάγκες του Ινστιτούτου για αίθουσα διαλέξεων και επιπλέον χώρους γραφείων ικανοποιήθηκαν λίγο αργότερα με την αγορά παρακείμενου οικοπέδου και την κατασκευή νέας πτέρυγας με χρηματοδότηση του Ιδρύματος Velux. Η νέα πτέρυγα εγκαινιάστηκε το 2000 και φιλοξενεί έκτοτε τις εκδηλώσεις του Ινστιτούτου. Το Ινστιτούτο νοικιάζει επίσης διαμέρισμα τεσσάρων δωματίων στη κοντινή οδό Παρθενώνος, το οποίο χρησιμοποιεί ως ξενώνα για φοιτητές.

The student hostel in Parthenonos 22.

Entering the Danish Institute one meets the secretary Hanna Lassen, who has been with the Institute since its inauguration.

View from the guesthouse in Herefondos 12.

Reception in the guesthouse after a formal lecture.

Institutet er udstyret med, hvad en græsk avis har kaldt "stylish substance": Møbler og andet inventar er gennemgående Dansk design repræsenteret med navne som Piet Hein, Arne Jacobsen, Poul Henningsen og Le Klint. På væggene finder man dansk kunst, som er deponeret af Ny Carlsbergfondet eller som er skænket af kunstnere, der har haft stipender ved Instituttet. Blandt kunstnerne kan nævnes Peter Brandes, Jes Fomsgaard og Hanne Sejrbo Nielsen.

The rooms at the Institute are furnished in what a Greek newspaper called "stylish substance". Furniture and lamps are all in Danish Design represented by names as Piet Hein, Arne Jacobsen, Poul Henningsen, and LeKlint. The walls are decorated with Danish art deposited from the Ny Carlsbergfondet or which has been donated by artists who held scholarships at the Institute. Among the artists can be mentioned Peter Brandes, Jes Fomsgaard and Hanne Sejrbo Nielsen.

Οι χώροι του Ινστιτούτου επιπλώθηκαν με "απλή κομψότητα", όπως το έθεσε ελληνική εφημερίδα. Έπιπλα και φωτιστικά υπογράφονται από Δανούς σχεδιαστές και κατασκευαστές όπως οι Piet Hein, Arne Jacobsen, Poul Henningsen και LeKlint, ενώ τους τοίχους κοσμούν έργα τέχνης διαφόρων καλλιτεχνών που παραχώρησε η Ny Carlsbergfondet. Από τους καλλιτέχνες αναφέρουμε ενδεικτικά τους Peter Brandes, Jes Fomsgaard και Hanne Sejrbo Nielsen.

# The Directors

Søren Dietz (1992-1997). The National Museum.

Signe Isager (1998-2000). University of Southern Denmark.

Jørgen Mejer (2001-2003). University of Copenhagen.

Erik Hallager (2004-present). University of Aarhus.

Instituttet er en selvejende institution under Ministeriet for Videnskab, Teknologi og Udvikling, og det har en bestyrelse på 10 medlemmer. Disse repræsenterer Udenrigs-, Kultur-, Undervisnings- og Videnskabsministerierne, de tre gamle universiteter, København, Aarhus og Syddansk samt Nationalmuseet og Akademiraadet og den til enhver tid siddende ambassadør i Grækenland. Bestyrelsen udpeger Instituttets direktør, som er ansvarlig for dets daglige drift. Instituttet finansieres med en hovedbevilling fra Videnskabsministeriet med betragtelige tilskud fra universiteterne og Nationalmuseet. Desuden sikres Instituttets overlevelse med tilskud fra Kulturministeriet og Undervisningsministeriet samt fra private fonde.

Instituttets faste stab har hidtil bestået af en direktør, en vicedirektør på deltid, to deltidssekretærer, en deltidsbogholder samt to græske medarbejdere.

The Institute is a self-governing institution under the Ministry of Science, Technology and Development. It consists of a board of directors with ten members who represent: the Ministries of Foreign Affairs, Culture, Education, and Science, the Universities of Copenhagen, Aarhus and Southern Denmark, the National Museum, the Academy Counsil and the ambassador of Denmark to Greece. The board appoints the director of the Institute, who is responsible for the day to day running. The Institute is financed mainly by the Ministry of Science with major contributions from the Universities and the National Museum. Further the survival of the Institute is secured by contributions from the Ministry of Education, the Ministry of Culture and private foundations.

The ordinary staff of the Institute consists of a director, a part time assistant director, two part time secretaries, a part time accountant as well as two Greek employees.

Το Ινστιτούτο είναι αυτοδιοικούμενο ίδρυμα που υπάγεται στο Υπουργείο Επιστημών, Τεχνολογίας και Ανάπτυξης. Το δεκαμελές διοικητικό του συμβούλιο εκπροσωπεύει τα Υπουργεία Εξωτερικών, Πολιτισμού, Παιδείας και Επιστημών της Δανίας, τα Πανεπιστήμια Κοπεγχάγης, Aarhus και Νότιας Δανίας, το Εθνικό Μουσείο, την Ακαδημαϊκό Συμβούλιο και τον εκάστοτε πρεσβή της Δανίας στην Αθήνα. Το Ινστιτούτο χρηματοδοτείται κατά κύριο λόγο από το Υπουργείο Επιστημών, και σε μικρότερο βαθμό από τα πανεπιστήμια και το Εθνικό Μουσείο. Επιπλέον χρηματοδότηση παρέχουν τα Υπουργεία Παιδείας και Πολιτισμού, καθώς και ιδιωτικά ιδρύματα.

Το προσωπικό του Ινστιτούτου αποτελείται από το διευθυντή, ο οποίος εκλέγεται από το διοικητικό συμβούλιο και φροντίζει για την εύρυθμη λειτουργία του Ινστιτούτου, τον υποδιευθυντή, δύο γραμματείς και ένα λογιστή μερικής απασχόλησης, καθώς και δύο Έλληνίδες υπαλλήλους.

# The Nordic Library

From the inauguration of the Nordic Library in October 1995.

A student at work in the Nordic Library. The library contains more than 40.000 volumes.

In celebration of the 10th anniversary of the Nordic Library a day of formal lectures by Nordic scholars was arranged. Presentations of their work were given in the Library. Ambassador Niels Henrik Sliben is seen addressing the participants on behalf of the Nordic embassies.

Noget af det vigtigste for besøgende forskere er gode biblioteksfaciliteter. I stedet for at etablere egne små biblioteker er det Svenske, Finske, Norske og Danske Institut gået sammen om at skabe et stort fælles Nordisk Bibliotek. Det har fungeret siden 1995, og det besøges af såvel nordiske som græske og andre udenlandske forskere og studerende.

One of the most important services a visiting scholar requires is good library facilities. Instead of establishing their own small libraries the Swedish, Finnish, Norwegian and Danish Institutes went together and established a large Nordic Library. It was established in 1995 and are frequented by Nordic, Greek and foreign scholars and students.

Μια από τις σημαντικότερες υπηρεσίες που μπορεί να προσφέρει ένα αρχαιολογικό ινστιτούτο στους ερευνητές είναι μια άρτια εξοπλισμένη βιβλιοθήκη. Τα σκανδιναβικά ινστιτούτα ίδρυσαν από κοινού τη Βιβλιοθήκη των Βορείων Χωρών. Η βιβλιοθήκη αυτή λειτουργεί από το 1995 και δέχεται φοιτητές και ερευνητές από τη Σκανδιναβία, την Ελλάδα και πολλές άλλες χώρες.

# International conferences, symposia, and workshops

The Danish National Research Foundation's Centre for Textile Research held its first international workshop at the Danish Institute.

The textile workshop also included practical experiments of weaving with replica Minoan loom weights. January 2006.

From a Minoan Seminar held in Mochlos, Crete 2005. The Minoan Seminars are an international forum for the discussion of current research in Minoan archaeology and have been organized by the Danish Institute since spring 2004.

På den videnskabelige front er Det Danske Institut aktivt med at arrangere internationale konferencer, symposier og workshops. De fleste bliver organiseret af Instituttet, mens andre er arrangeret i samarbejde med græske institutioner eller andre udenlandske skoler. Mange konferencer er desuden publiceret af Det Danske Institut.

Instituttet er ofte vært for og

On the scientific front the Danish Institute is actively arranging International conferences, symposia and workshops. Most of these are organized by the Institute itself, whilst others are arranged in collaboration with Greek Institutions or with other foreign Institutes. Most proceedings are also published by the Danish Institute.

The Institute hosts and often co-

Σε ό,τι αφορά το επιστημονικό του έργο, το Ινστιτούτο διοργανώνει τακτικά διεθνή συνέδρεια, συμπόσια και ημερίδες, είτε μόνο του, είτε σε συνεργασία με ελληνικούς φορείς ή άλλα ξένα ινστιτούτα. Τα πεπραγμένα των συναντήσεων αυτών εκδίδονται συνήθως από το Ινστιτούτο της Δανίας.

Επιπλέον, το Ινστιτούτο διοργανώνει σε συνεργασία με άλλους φο-

# Ph.d. seminars, internal seminars, and formal lectures

From a Ph.D. seminar on "Early Christianity in Athens" partly organized by the Danish Institute in 2005.

The participants of the Ph.D. seminar are guided by Guy Sanders at Corinth.

From an internal "Holberg seminar" where the artist Karen Degett presented and discussed her work at the Institute 2006.

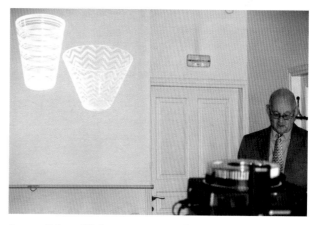

Jørgen Schou-Christensen presented in 2005 the first formal lecture in a series concerning modern Danish Design.

medarrangør af Ph.d. seminarer fra de hjemlige forskerskoler. Vi giver også besøgende forskere, studenter og kunstnere mulighed for at præsentere resultaterne af deres studier på interne "Holberg-seminarer". Herudover arrangerer Instituttet mange offentlige forelæsninger over emner, som kan være af interesse i det græske og internationale miljø i Athen.

organizes educational programmes for Ph.D. students from research centres in Denmark. We also provide visiting scholars, students and artists with opportunity to present results from their studies at internal "Holberg seminars". Furthermore the Institute arranges many public lectures on topics of intererest to the Greek and international communities in Athens.

ρείς προγράμματα για φοιτητές διδακτορικού επιπέδου και παρέχει τη δυνατότητα στους φιλοξενούμενους ερευνητές, φοιτητές και καλλιτέχνες να παρουσιάσουν τα αποτελέσματα της δουλειάς τους στο Ινστιτούτο. Το Ινστιτούτο διοργανώνει επίσης πλήθος διαλέξεων πάνω σε θέματα ποικίλου ενδιαφέροντος, που απευθύνονται τόσο σε Έλληνες όσο και σε ξένους της Αθήνας.

# Cultural events

In 1993 the Danish Institute initiated a pilot-project on pithos making in Thrapsano, Crete. The Danish potter Per Weiss is on the left.

View from the exhibition "Reflections" with paintings and sculptures, held in the guesthouse in 2000.

One of the major cultural events at the Danish Institute was the Helios Festival in 2000 with performances by Carl Nielsen's music (here in Technopolis) along with an exhibition of his wife Anne Marie Carl Nielsen's works of art, inspired by Greek surroundings during their stay in Greece in 1903 and 1904.

Det Danske Institut har også til opgave at drive kulturformidling. Instituttets direktør er desuden kulturråd ved den danske ambassade. De kulturelle arrangementer, som har til formål at udbygge de kulturelle forbindelser mellem Danmark og Grækenland, er mangesidige. De strækker sig fra begivenheder i Instituttets faciliteter med koncer-

The Danish Institute encourages general cultural exchange. The Director of the Institute is also cultural counsellor at the Danish Embassy. The cultural events, the main purpose of which is to strengthen cultural relations between Denmark and Greece, are multifaceted. They may be events run in the lecture hall at the Institute such

Το Ινστιτούτο υποστηρίζει και προωθεί τις πολιτιστικές ανταλλαγές. Ο διευθυντής του είναι και μορφωτικός σύμβουλος της Πρεσβείας της Δανίας στην Ελλάδα και οι πολυσχιδείς δραστηριότητές του έχουν σαν στόχο την ενίσχυση των δανο-ελληνικών πολιτιστικών σχέσεων. Οι δραστηριότητες αυτές - συναυλίες, ομιλίες, εκθέσεις - λαμ-

# Cultural events

The Hans Christian Andersen celebrations pre-started in 2003 with the Danish actress Githa Nørby reading fairy tales at the Institute, whilst the Hans Christian Andersen ambassador, Mrs. Niki Goulandri in 2005 inaugurated an exhibition which then traveled all over Greece.

The Danish Institute has since 1993 sponsored the participation of Danish bands in Athens' International Jazz Festival – the first year saw the Arne Forchammer's trio. The Institute also organises numerous musical events, held in the lecture hall. Here with Vini Iuel and Thomas Clausen with his Brazilian Trio.

ter, foredrag, udstillinger og meget andet til kulturelle begivenheder, som huses i Athens store koncertsale, gallerier, museer og dansescener eller som gennemføres andre steder i Grækenland. Desuden bestræber vi os på, at Danmark også er repræsenteret ved større internationale kulturelle begivenheder.

as concerts, lectures, exhibitions, and the like. Other cultural events have taken place in concert halls, galleries, museums and dancing scenes at various locations in Athens, and throughout Greece. Furthermore we try to secure that Denmark is represented at larger international cultural events.

βάνουν χώρα είτε στην αίθουσα διαλέξεων του Ινστιτούτου, είτε σε άλλους χώρους, όπως αίθουσες συναυλιών, μουσεία, γκαλερί και θέατρα, σε όλη την Ελλάδα. Το Ινστιτούτο φροντίζει επίσης ώστε η Δανία να εκπροσωπείται στις μεγάλες διεθνείς πολιτιστικές εκδηλώσεις.

# Publications of the Institute

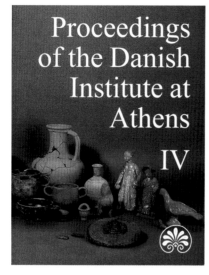

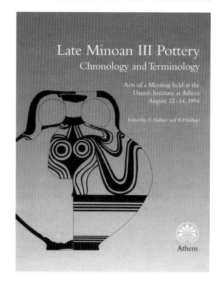

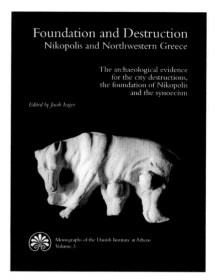

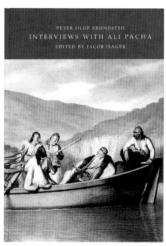

A few selected publications from the Danish Institute. Upper row a periodical and two monographs, lower row, two works from the Miscelleneous series - the first on Ali Pasha and the second on the Sarakatsans. Finally a report on the activity by the Institute 1992-1993.

Det Danske Institut udgiver tre publikationer: tidsskriftet *Proceedings of the Danish Institute at Athens* (PDIA), monografiserien *Monographs of the Danish Institute at Athens* MDIA), med kongres- og udgravningsrapporter samt en serie med mere individuelle publikationer over emner med fælles dansk-græsk berøring. Publikationerne redigeres af Instituttets akademiske personale.

The Danish Institute issues three series of publications; a periodical *Proceedings of the Danish Institute at Athens* (PDIA), a monograph series *Monographs of the Danish Institute at Athens* (MDIA) with congress and excavation reports; and a miscellaneous series with topics on common Greek-Danish relations. The publications are edited by the academic staff at the Institute.

Το Ινστιτούτο εκδίδει τρεις σειρές: το περιοδικό *Proceedings of the Danish Institute at Athens* (PDIA), τη σειρά *Monographs of the Danish Institute at Athens* (MDIA), στην οποία δημοσιεύονται πεπραγμένα συνεδρίων και ανασκαφικές εκθέσεις, και μια γενική σειρά με θέματα που αφορούν στις δανο-ελληνικές σχέσεις. Τις εκδόσεις αυτές επιμελείται το επιστημονικό προσωπικό του Ινστιτούτου.

# Instituttets arkæologiske projekter
# The archaeological projects by the Institute
# Αρχαιολογικά προγράμματα του Ινστιτούτου

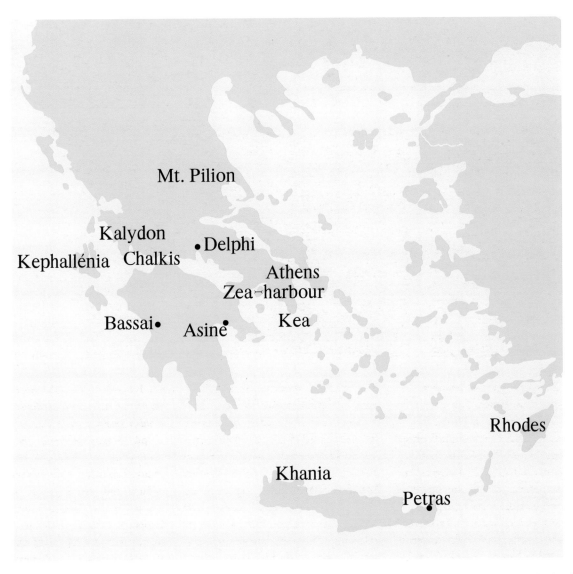

Mt. Pilion

Kalydon

Kephallénia   Chalkis   •Delphi

Athens

Zea-harbour

Bassai•   Asine•   Kea

Rhodes

Khania

Petras

Sites with red dots are those represented at the exhibition while the others are only presented or mentioned in this book.

# Kephallenia

Assos with a Venetian castle.

Kato Katelios where an ancient harbour was identified.

Pyrgos with remains of an ancient fortification wall.

Det første projekt i Instituttets regie var et survey på den østlige del af øen Kefallenia. Det blev fra dansk side ledet af professor Klavs Randsborg og fra græsk side af Dr. Lazaros Kolonas, daværende efor i Patras. Projektet begyndte i virkeligheden i 1991 som en græsk-svensk undersøgelse, men med etableringen af det Danske Institut i 1992 overgik det til et græsk-dansk projekt. Det blev afsluttet i 1994 og den endelige publikation i to bind forelå i 2002.

The first project for the new Institute was a survey in the eastern part of Kephallenia. Professor Klavs Randsborg conducted the Danish team. The project was run in collaboration with Dr. Lazaros Kolonas, the then ephor in Patras. The project started in 1991 as a Greek-Swedish enterprise but with the establishment of the Danish Institute in 1992 it became a Greek-Danish project. It lasted until 1994. The publication, of two volumes, was published in 2002.

Το πρώτο πρόγραμμα του νεοσυσταθέντος Ινστιτούτου ήταν η επιφανειακή έρευνα στην ανατολική Κεφαλλονιά υπό τη διεύθυνση του καθηγητή Klaus Randsborg. Το πρόγραμμα ξεκίνησε το 1991 σαν ελληνοσουηδική αποστολή σε συνεργασία με τον Δρ. Λάζαρο Κολώνα, τότε προϊστάμενο της Εφορείας Αρχαιοτήτων Πάτρας. Με την ίδρυση του Ινστιτούτου της Δανίας το 1992, η αποστολή μετονομάστηκε σε ελληνοδανική. Το πρόγραμμα διήρκεσε έως το 1994 και η τελική έκθεσή του κυκλοφόρησε σε δύο τόμους το 2002.

# Rhodes

The Archaic settlement of Vroulia as seen from the east.

Remains from an amphora kiln.

Members of the survey team in action.

Instituttets næste projekt var et græsk-dansk survey på det sydlige Rhodos i 1994. Det blev fra dansk side ledet af dr. phil. Søren Dietz og fra græsk side af Dr. Efi Karantzali. Formålet med surveyet var blandt andet at undersøge detaljer og spørgsmål, som var blevet rejst i publikationerne af den gamle danske Rhodos-ekspedition i begyndelsen af århundredet. Resultaterne er under bearbejdning.

The next project by the Institute was a Greek-Danish Survey in southern Rhodes in 1994. Dr. Søren Dietz led the Danish team whilst Dr. Efi Karantzali led the Greek. The survey aimed to explore further details and questions raised from the publication of the previous Danish Expedition at Rhodes at the beginning of the century. The results of this survey are now under study.

Ακολούθησε η επιφανειακή έρευνα στη νότια Ρόδο, μια ελληνο-δανική συνεργασία υπό τη διεύθυνση του Δρ. Σόρεν Dietz, από πλευράς Ινστιτούτου, και της Δρ. Έφης Καράντζαλη από την εφορεία αρχαιοτήτων Ρόδου. Στόχος του προγράμματος ήταν η περαιτέρω διερεύνηση ερωτημάτων που έθεσε προηγούμενη έρευνα. Τα αποτελέσματα της έρευνας αυτής βρίσκονται στο στάδιο της μελέτης.

# Chalkis, Aitolias

The mound of Chalkis as seen from the east. The site of Pangali lies on the terrace slopes of Mount Varassova, behind the mound.

Chalkis er en af de fem byer i Aitolien, som Homer fortæller deltog i den Trojanske Krig. Byen omtales ligeledes af historieskriveren Thukydid. De græsk-danske udgravninger i Chalkis, der varede fra1995 til 2001, blev ledet af Dr. Lazaros Kolonas og dr. phil. Søren Dietz. To lokaliteter blev undersøgt. Pangali-bakken på Varassovabjergets skråning havde betydelige fund fra den sene stenalder og rester af en klassisk forsvarsmur blev identificeret. På Hagia Triada-højen blev tre områder med levn fra bronzealderen ned til byzantinsk tid udgravet. Udgravningerne er i øjeblikket under endelig publicering og første bind udkom i april 2006.

Chalkis is counted by Homer as one of the five Aitolian cities which took part in the Trojan War, it is also mentioned by the ancient historianThucydides. The Greek-Danish excavations in Chalkis between 1995-2001 were under the direction of Dr. Lazaros Kolonas and Dr. Søren Dietz. Two localities were investigated. The Pangali hill on the Varassova mountain, with important finds from the Neolithic period and remains of a classical fortification. On the Hagia Triada hill three areas with remains from the Bronze Age to the Byzantine period were unearthed. The excavation results are being published with the first volume out in 2006.

Στη Χαλκίδα, μια από τις πέντε αιτωλικές πόλεις που, κατά τον Όμηρο, εκστράτευσαν εναντίον της Τροίας και η οποία αναφέρεται και από τον Θουκυδίδη, οι ελληνοδανικές ανασκαφές υπό τους Δρ. Λάζαρο Κολώνα και Søren Dietz διήρκεσαν από το 1995 ως το 2001. Ερευνήθηκαν δύο χώροι: ο λόφος Παγκάλη στα βουνά της Βαράσσοβας, με τα σημαντικά νεολιθικά κατάλοιπα και τα λείψανα οχύρωσης των κλασικών χρόνων, και ο λόφος Αγίας Τριάδας, όπου ανασκάφτηκαν τρεις τομείς με κατάλοιπα της Εποχής του Χαλκού και των Βυζαντινών χρόνων. Ο πρώτος τόμος της ανασκαφικής έκθεσης κυκλοφόρησε το 2006.

Assemblage of obsidian and chert tools from the Neolithic settlement at Pangali.

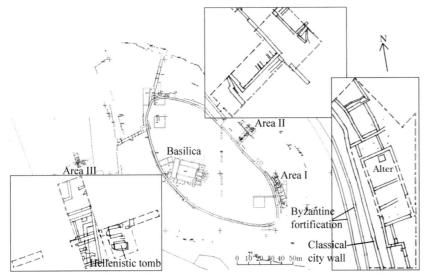

Plan of the mound of Chalkis with details of the three excavated areas.

Archaic foundations and prehistoric soundings in Area II west of the mound.

Chalkis Aitolias I
The prehistoric periods

Edited by *Søren Dietz & Ioannis Moschos*

Monographs of the Danish Institute at Athens,
Volume 7

Volume 1 of the Chalkis excavations publication edited by Søren Dietz and Ioannis Moschos. Published in 2006.

Finds from the Hellenistic tomb in Area II.

# Kalydon, Aitolias

View from the eastern gate of Kalydon towards the Evinos river.

Mens de gamle græsk-danske udgravninger i Kalydon var koncentreret til området uden for bymuren, kom de genoptagne udgravninger i 2000 til 2005 under ledelse af dr. phil. Søren Dietz og Dr. Ioannis Moschos til at lægge hovedvægten på undersøgelser inden for bymuren. Her blev der gennemført et storstilet geomagnetisk survey, som afslørede den antikke byplan. Udgravninger på byens akropol viste lag fra arkaisk og klassisk tid, mens en bygning med en helligdom samt en keramikovn blev udgravet inden for vestporten. Uden for bymuren blev der fundet et unikt teater med firkantet orkestra.

While the old Greek-Danish excavations at Kalydon had concentrated on the area outside the city wall the resumption of the excavations (2000-2005) under the direction of Dr. Søren Dietz and Dr. Ioannis Moschos has mainly concentrated on the remains inside the city walls. Here a large-scale geomagnetic survey has exposed the city plan. The excavations have revealed important Archaic and Classical remains on the Acropolis. Inside the western gate a building with a shrine was found. Further excavations outside the city wall were conducted in what proved to be a unique theatre with a squarish orchestra.

Σε αντίθεση με τις παλαιότερες ελληνο-δανικές ανασκαφές στην αρχαία Καλυδώνα Αιτωλίας, οι οποίες επικεντρώθηκαν στην περιοχή εκτός των τειχών, οι νεώτερες έρευνες (2000-2005), υπό τη διεύθυνση των Δρ. Γιάννη Μόσχου και Søren Dietz, εστιάστηκαν στην περιοχή εντός των τειχών, όπου εκτενής γεωφυσική έρευνα αποκάλυψε το πολεοδομικό σχέδιο της πόλης. Οι ανασκαφές έφεραν στο φως σημαντικά λείψανα της Αρχαϊκής και Κλασικής εποχής στην περιοχή της ακρόπολης. Εντός της δυτικής πύλης αποκαλύφτηκε κτίριο με ιερό, ενώ εκτός των τοιχών ανασκάφτηκε ασυνήθιστο θέατρο με παραλληλόγραμμη ορχήστρα.

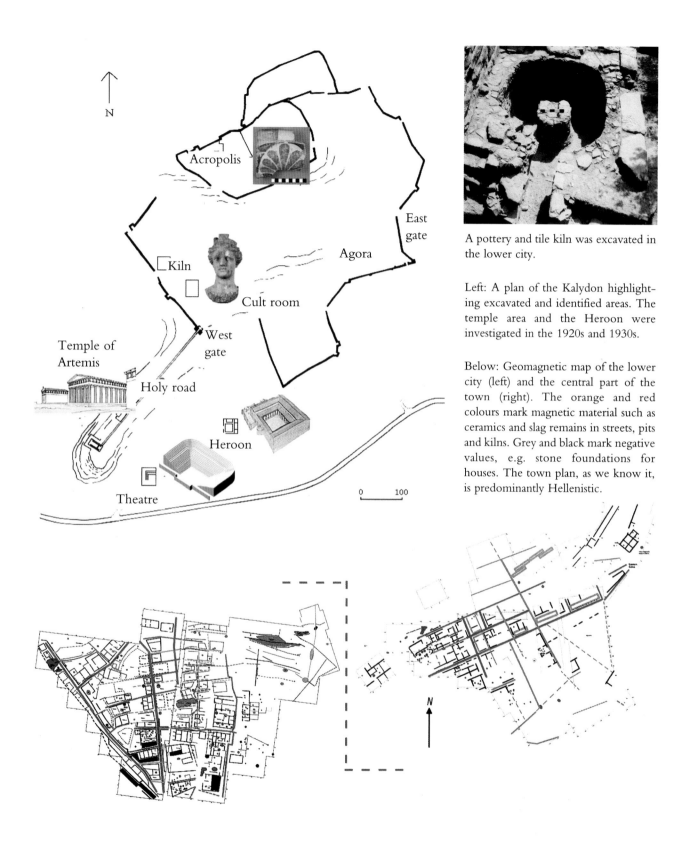

Acropolis

East gate

Agora

Kiln

Cult room

West gate

Temple of Artemis

Holy road

Heroon

Theatre

0    100

A pottery and tile kiln was excavated in the lower city.

Left: A plan of the Kalydon highlighting excavated and identified areas. The temple area and the Heroon were investigated in the 1920s and 1930s.

Below: Geomagnetic map of the lower city (left) and the central part of the town (right). The orange and red colours mark magnetic material such as ceramics and slag remains in streets, pits and kilns. Grey and black mark negative values, e.g. stone foundations for houses. The town plan, as we know it, is predominantly Hellenistic.

N

# Zea Harbour Project, Pireaus

Instituttets seneste igangværende udgravning er de kombinerede land- og undervandsudgravninger i Zea-havnen i Piræus. Projektet begyndte i 2001, og er fra dansk side ledet af Bjørn Lovén og fra græsk side af Dr. Aik. Delaporta (2001-2006) og Dr. Cha. Pennas (2006), for undervandseforatet samt af Dr. G. Steinhauer (2001-2005), Dr. E. Konsolakis (2005-2006) og Dr. E. Lygouri (2006) for det 26. Eforat. Projektet er finansieret af Carlsbergfondet.

Projektets formål er at undersøge Zeas havneinstallationer og forsvarsværker i klassisk og hellenistisk tid. Skibshusene rummede 196 triremer og dækkede et areal på mere end 55.000m². De var blandt de største og vigtigste bygningskomplekser i klassisk tid.

The most recent excavation by the Danish Institute is the combined land and underwater excavations at the Zea harbour. The project, which began in 2001, is directed by Mr. Bjørn Lovén for the Danish Institute. The Greek directors are Dr. Aik. Delaporta (2001-2006), Dr. Cha. Pennas (2006) from the Underwater Ephorate and Dr. G. Steinhauer (2001-2005), Dr. E. Konsolakis (2005-2006) and Dr. E. Lygouri (2006) from the 26th Ephorate.

The aim of the project is to investigate the remains of the harbour installations and fortifications of Zea from the Classical and Hellenistic periods. The shipsheds housed some 196 triremes and covered more than 55.000 m². They were one of the largest building complexes of the Classical period.

Ένα από τα πιο πρόσφατα ερευνητικά προγράμματα του Ινστιτούτου αφορά στις χερσαίες και υποβρύχιες ανασκαφές στο λιμάνι της Ζέας. Το πρόγραμμα ξεκίνησε το 2001 με διευθυντές τον Bjørn Lovén από πλευράς Ινστιτούτου, τους Δρ. Αικ. Δελαπόρτα (2001-2006) και Χαρ. Πέννα (2006) της Εφορείας Εναλίων Αρχαιοτήτων και τους Δρ. Γ. Σταϊνχαουερ (2001-2005), Ε. Κονσολάκη (2005-2006) και Ευτ. Λυγκούρη (2006) της ΚΣΤ΄ Εφορείας Αρχαιοτήτων. Στόχος του προγράμματος είναι η διερεύνηση των κλασικών και ελληνιστικών λειψάνων των λιμενικών εγκαταστάσεων και της οχύρωσης της Ζέας. Οι νεώσοικοι της Ζέας κάλυπταν έκταση 55 στρεμμάτων και μπορούσαν να στεγάσουν περί τις 196 τριήρεις. Πρόκειται για το μεγαλύτερο γνωστό κτιριακό συγκρότημα της Κλασικής εποχής.

Archaeologist inspecting the rock-cut features that held transverse timbers on the ramp of a shipshed. The reason why excavations must also be carried out in the sea is that the sea level has risen *c.* 2 m. since antiquity and thus submerged the lower part of the shipsheds.

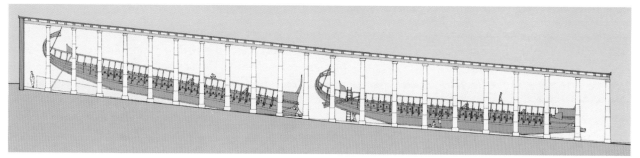

The project has established that double-shipsheds lined Zea's eastern shore in the 4th century BC.

It took 140 men to haul a trireme into a shipshed.

# Mt. Pilion Cave Project

Above: Cave featuring a small chapel. Right: Lowland animal enclosure constructed around a small cave at the edge of lake Karla.

Instituttets nye projekt, Pilion hule-projektet i Volos-regionen, er planlagt til at begynde i efteråret 2006. Det er et samarbejde mellem eforatet for paleoantropologi og huleforskning i Nordgrækenland under Dr. Efi Poulaki og Det Danske Institut i Athen repræsenteret ved cand.mag. Niels Andreasen.

Projektets formål er at undersøge og beskrive de mangeartede aktiviteter, der har foregået i og omkring huler i senere historiske perioder og i moderne tid. Projektet vil integrere arkæologi, historie og socialantropologi i et interdisiplinært samarbejde og indhente informationer ved hjælp af systematiske overflade-indsamlinger, lokal historisk forskning samt interviews med lokale beboere.

The latest project run by the Institute is the Pilion Cave Project in the Volos region, planned to start in 2006. It is a co-operation between the ephorate for Palaeoanthropology and Cave Research in Northern Greece under Dr. Efi Poulaki and the Danish Institute at Athens represented by Niels Andreasen, MA.

The purpose of the project is to develop a more representative picture of the activities inside and around caves during the latter historical and modern periods. The project integrates archaeology, history and social anthropology within an interdisiplinary framework and will obtain its information through surveys, local history research and interviews with local recidents.

Το Πρόγραμμα Σπηλαίων Πηλίου, το πιο πρόσφατο ερευνητικό πρόγραμμα του Ινστιτούτου, θα ξεκινήσει το 2006 από τον Niels Andreasen και τη Δρ. Έφη Πουλάκη της Εφορείας Παλαιοανθρωπολογίας και Σπηλαιολογίας Βόρειας Ελλάδας.

Στόχος του προγράμματος είναι η καταγραφή των δραστηριοτήτων που λάμβαναν χώρα μέσα και γύρω από τα σπήλαια αυτά στην ύστερη ιστορική και νεώτερη εποχή. Το πρόγραμμα συνδυάζει αρχαιολογία, ιστορία και κοινωνική ανθρωπολογία και στηρίζεται για τη συλλογή των απαιτούμενων πληροφοριών στη συστηματική περισυλλογή επιφανειακών ευρημάτων, την ιστορική έρευνα σε τοπικό επίπεδο και σε συνεντεύξεις με τους ντόπιους.

# Akademisk ansattes projekter
# Projects by the academic staff
# Προγράμματα του επιστημονικού προσωπικού

Det videnskabelige akademiske personale på Det Danske Institut i Athen har indtil nu bestået af en direktør og en vicedirektør. Instituttets første direktør, dr.phil. Søren Dietz, er arkæolog og arbejder stadig i Grækenland. Den følgende direktør, lektor Signe Isager er antikhistoriker med speciale i græsk epigrafik, mens den tredje, dr.phil Jørgen Mejer, er klassisk filolog med speciale i græsk drama og filosofi.

Den nuværende direktør er adjungeret professor, dr. phil. Erik Hallager, som i øjeblikket er engageret i to arkæologiske projekter. Det ene er de fortsatte græsk-svenske udgravninger i Khania og den endelige publikation af udgravningerne fra årene 1970-87 og 2001. Det andet er publiceringen af et arkiv med kretiske hieroglyffer fundet i Petras i 1996 og 1997 sammen med udgraveren Dr. Metaxia Tsipopoulou.

Den nuværende vicedirektør, cand.phil. Jesper Jensen, er ved at afslutte sin Ph.d. om Asklepeion på Akropolis' sydskråning, hvor han har genfundet et tempel for Asklepios. Desuden arbejder han sammen med Dr. Fanis Mavridis på en stor antologi om huler i Grækenland.

The scientific and academic staff of the Danish Institute has until now consisted of a director and an assistant director. The first director Dr. Phil. Søren Dietz is an archaeologist and still works in Greece. Subsequently, former director Signe Isager is an atiqiuty historian who specialised in Greek epigraphy, while the third, Dr. Phil. Jørgen Mejer is a Classical philologist specialised in Greek drama and philosophy.

The current director is Honorary Professor, Dr. Phil. Erik Hallager, who is presently involved in two archaeological projects. One is the Greek-Swedish Excavations at Khania which includes the final publication of the excavation from the years 1970-87 and 2001. The other is a joint publication with the excavator Dr. Metaxia Tzipopoulou of an archive containing Cretan hieroglyphs found at Petras in 1996/1997.

The current assistant director is Jesper Jensen, MA, who is finishing his Ph.D. about the Asklepeion in Athens, where he has re-discovered a temple for Asklepios. Furthermore he works in collaboration with Dr. Fanis Mavridis on a large anthology about the caves of Greece.

Το επιστημονικό και ακαδημαϊκό προσωπικό του Ινστιτούτου αποτελείται από το διευθυντή και τον υποδιευθυντή. Πρώτος διευθυντής του Ινστιτούτου διετέλεσε ο αρχαιολόγος Δρ. Søren Dietz, ο οποίος εξακολουθεί να εργάζεται στην Ελλάδα. Τον διαδέχτηκε η Signe Isager, καθηγήτρια αρχαίας ιστορίας με ειδίκευση στην ελληνική επιγραφική, ενώ τρίτος διευθυντής διετέλεσε ο Δρ. Jørgen Mejer, κλασικός φιλόλογος με ειδίκευση στο ελληνικό θέατρο και την ελληνική φιλοσοφία.

Ο εν ενεργεία διευθυντής του Ινστιτούτου και επίτιμος καθηγητής Erik Hallager συμμετέχει σε δύο αρχαιολογικά προγράμματα: τις ελληνο-σουηδικές ανασκαφές Χανίων, των οποίων ετοιμάζει τις τελικές ανασκαφικές εκθέσεις για τα έτη 1970-87 και 2001, και την από κοινού δημοσίευση αρχείου Κρητικής Ιερογλυφικής από τον Πετρά Σητείας (1996-97) με την ανασκαφέα του αρχείου Δρ. Μεταξία Τσιποπούλου.

Ο υποδιευθυντής του Ινστιτούτου Jesper Jensen ολοκληρώνει τη διδακτορική διατριβή του με θέμα το Ασκληπιείο της Νοτίου Κλιτύος της Ακρόπολης, όπου ανακάλυψε άγνωστη μέχρι τώρα φάση του ναού του Ασκληπιού. Ετοιμάζει επίσης εκτενή ανθολογία των ελληνικών σπηλαίων σε συνεργασία με το Φάνη Μαυρίδη.

# Khania, western Crete

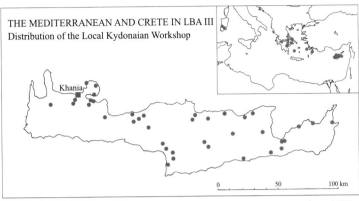

THE MEDITERRANEAN AND CRETE IN LBA III
Distribution of the Local Kydonaian Workshop

Khania

0      50      100 km

The pottery from the Kydonian Workshop of the LM III period, *c.* 1400-1200, was distributed all over Crete and in the Mediterranean.

Unusual straight-sided stirrup jar from the Kydonian workshop. LM IIIB:2, *c.* 1200.

De græsk-svenske udgravninger på Ag. Aikaterini pladsen på Kastellihøjen i Khania har siden 1969 været ledet af Dr. Yannis Tzedakis. Leder for den svenske del er professor Carl-Gustaf Styrenius. De tekniske udgravningsledere er dr.phil. Erik Hallager (siden 1972) og Dr. Maria Vlazaki.

Udgravningerne er meget vigtige, da de dækker 5000 år af byens historie. Vigtigheden bevidnes ligeledes af mange fund af dokumenter fra såvel den minoiske Linear A som den mykenske Linear B administration samt af de ikke mindre end syv stratificerede bebyggelseslag, der findes fra den senminoiske periode (ca. 1600-1150 f.Kr.) Resultaterne fra udgravningerne har sammen med de græske udgravninger på Kastellihøjen og i Splantzia kvarteret uden al tvivl vist betydningen af den minoiske bebyggelse i Khania som et af de vigtigste paladscentre på Kreta.

The Greek-Swedish Excavations (GSE) in the Ag. Aikaterini Square, on the Kastelli Hill of the town of Khania, has been ongoing since 1969, under the general direction of Dr. Yannis Tzedakis. Director of the Swedish team is Professor Carl-Gustav Styrenius. Field directors are Dr. Erik Hallager (since 1972) and Dr. Maria Vlazaki.

The excavation is very important, as it spans 5000 years of the town's history. It is furthermore witnessed by the finds of many documents of both the Minoan Linear A and the Mycenaean Linear B administration and by the seven layers of habitation through the Late Minoan period (c. 1600–1150 BC.). The results of the GSE in the Ag. Aikaterini Square and the Greek Excavations on the Kastelli Hill and in the Splantzia Quarter signify the great importance of the Minoan settlement of Khania as one of the most powerful palatial centres in Crete.

Η ελληνοσουηδική ανασκαφή στην Πλατεία Αγ. Αικατερίνης, στο λόφο Καστέλλι της πόλης των Χανιών ξεκίνησε το 1969 υπό τη γενική διεύθυνση του Δρ. Γιάννη Τζεδάκη. Διευθυντής της σουδικής ομάδας είναι ο καθηγητής Carl-Gustav Styrenius. Επικεφαλής των ανασκαφικών εργασιών είναι ο Δρ. Erik Hallager (από το 1972) και η Δρ. Μαρία Βλαζάκη.

Η ανασκαφή είναι ιδιαίτερα σημαντική, καθώς καλύπτει 5000 χρόνια ιστορίας της πόλης των Χανίων. Έχει φέρει στο φως πλήθος διοικητικών εγγράφων στη Γραμμικής Α και Β γραφή και έχει αποκαλύψει επτά διαφορετικά στρώματα κατοίκησης της Ύστερης Μινωικής περιόδου (περ. 1600-1150 π.Χ.). Τα αποτελέσματα της ελληνοσουηδικής ανασκαφής στην Πλατεία Αγ. Αικατερίνης και των ελληνικώ ανασκαφών στο λόφο Καστέλλι και τη συνοικία Σπλάντζιας καταδεικνύουν τη σημασία της μινωικής εγκατάστασης των Χανιών ως ενός από τα μεγάλα ανακτορικά κέντρα της Κρητής.

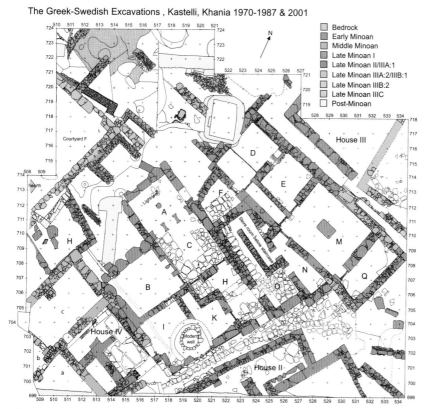

The Greek-Swedish Excavations , Kastelli, Khania 1970-1987 & 2001

Bedrock
Early Minoan
Middle Minoan
Late Minoan I
Late Minoan II/IIIA:1
Late Minoan IIIA:2/IIIB:1
Late Minoan IIIB:2
Late Minoan IIIC
Post-Minoan

Plan of the excavation showing the now visible remains through 5000 years.

*The Master Impression* is an image from a large gold ring impressed on a unique sealing found within the Minoan Linear A administration. The scene depicts a ruler or god on top of a fortified settlement by the sea. It had sealed a large document written on parchment.

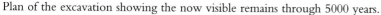

Stone vase, *c.* 1450 BC.

Amulet, *c.* 1450 BC.

Die, *c.* 1200 BC.

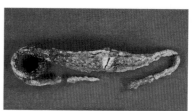

Fibula, *c.* 1150 BC.

A Linear B tablet found at a rescue excavation in 1990 on a floor dated to the end of the LM IIIB:1 period *c.* 1250 BC and proved for the first time that Dionysos was already a god in the Bronze Age. In translation the inscription reads: "To the shrine of Zeus: Zeus 1[+] jar of honey; to Dionysos 2 jars of honey".

# The re-discovered temple

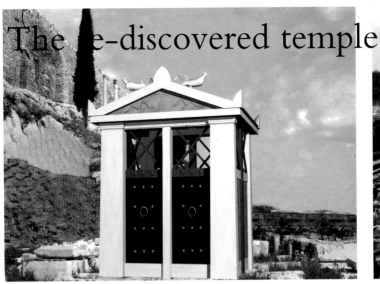

Reconstruction of the Asklepios temple.

The Asklepios sanctuary.

Den athenske helligdom for læge-guden Asklepios ligger på sydsiden af Athens Akropolis. Michalis Lefantzis og Jesper Jensen har i over to år arbejdet på en rekonstruktion af et lille tempel med tre byggefaser dateret til perioden 418-360 f.Kr. Et grundigt studie af alle de blokke, der hører til fundamentet af, hvad forskere tidligere har troet var et alter, og alle de fragmenter, der i dag ligger spredt ud over hellig-dommen, har ført til en sensationel opdagelse: I stedet for et helt alter har de to forskere fundet det første Asklepios-tempel. Da de havde rekonstrueret templet, viste det sig, at det også er gengivet på det såkaldte Telemachos-monument, der beskriver begyndelsen af hellig-dommens historie fra dens grundlæggelse i 420 til 412 f.Kr. Endvidere er det lille tempel omtalt i en anden indskrift, hvor det be-nævnes som *archaîos naós* (det gamle tempel).

The Athenian sanctuary of Askle-pios lies on the Southern Slope of the Akropolis. For more than two years Michalis Lefantzis and Jesper Jensen have worked on a recon-struction of a small temple showing three construction phases dated to the period 418-360 BC. A meticu-lous analysis of all the blocks belonging to what was originally believed to be an altar and all the other architectural blocks related to this monument, which were spread around the sanctuary, has resulted in a breathtaking discovery: Instead of finding a whole altar, the two scholars discovered the remains of the first temple at the sanctuary. Later they realized that the temple is depicted on the Telemachos Mo-nument which describes the early history of the sanctuary from 420 until 411 BC. Furthermore, the small temple is mentioned in a second inscription as *archaîos naós* (old temple).

Για περισσότερα από δύο χρόνια οι Μιχάλης Λεφαντζής και Jesper Jen-sen εργάζονται για την ανασύσταση μικρού ναού στο Ασκληπιείο της Νοτίου Κλιτύος της Ακρόπολης στην Αθήνα. Ο ναός αυτός παρου-σιάζει τρεις οικοδομικές φάσεις, οι οποίες χρονολογούνται από το 418 ως το 360 π.Χ. Η προσεκτική με-λέτη των δόμων που είχαν χρη-σιμοποιηθεί για την ανακατασκευή βωμού, αλλά και άλλων αρχι-τεκτονικών μελών που βρέθηκαν διάσπαρτα στο ιερό, οδήγησε στη συναρπαστική ανακάλυψη ότι οι δόμοι και τα μέλη αυτά ανήκαν στον πρώτο ναό του ιερού και όχι στον υποτιθέμενο βωμό. Οι ίδιοι ερευνητές ανακάλυψαν ότι ο πρώ-τος αυτός ναός εικονίζεται στο Μνημείο του Τηλέμαχου, το οποίο διηγείται την πρώιμη ιστορία του ιερού από το 420 ως το 411 π.Χ. Ο ναός αυτός αναφέρεται και σε δεύτερη επιγραφή ως "αρχαίος ναός".

# Catalogue of exhibits

Archaeological finds

Works of art

# Chalkis, Aitolias

1. Kantharos
Exc. no. F99-5015
Late 4$^{th}$ to 3$^{rd}$ cent. BC. Hellenistic
H 6.9 cm.

Black gloss surface, two vertical strap handles and splayed out-turned ring foot.

I.M. & S.D.

2. Spouted situla (filter jug for pouring wine)
Exc. no. F99-5014
Late 4$^{th}$ to early 3$^{rd}$ cent. BC. Hellenistic.
H 13 cm (including handle 18,6 cm).

Very worn. Spout in form of moulded lion's head. Basket handle attached to rim at spout and rear of jug.

I.M. & S.D.

3. Terracotta figurine
Exc. no. F99-5008
Early 3$^{rd}$ cent. BC. Hellenistic.
H 16.2 cm.

Tanagra figurine. Standing girl holding ball between right hand and hip, a rope or net folded over left wrist, fist clenched. Pink paint on flesh; blue on rope, white on chiton and red on hair. Hollow figurine, square opening carved in back.

I.M. & S.D.

4. Bronze mirror with lid
Exc. no. F99-5034
Late 4<sup>th</sup> to early 3<sup>rd</sup> cent. BC. Early Hellenistic.
D of lid 12.4 cm.

Restored from a total of five fragments. Bronze medusa head protome on lid.

I.M. & S.D.

# Kalydon, Aitolias

5

6

6. Lion
Agrinion Inv. no. 341,
Exc. no. F03-2164
2nd cent. BC.
H 55 cm.

## From

## Cultroom

5. Head of a cult statue
Agrinion Inv. no. 336,
Exc. no. F03-2163
2nd cent. BC.
H 41 cm.

The town goddess of Kalydon. The marble originates from the Cycladic islands, Paros or Naxos. The head of the goddess is slightly bent forward. On her head she carries a mural crown – a corona muralis – with four bastions(?). Her long curly hair waves slightly backwards from a centre parting and covers the upper part of both ears. Her hair is gathered in a bun at the back of her head. The shape of her face is oval with deep-set almond-shaped eyes, a finely rounded nose and a slightly open mouth with full lips. She has two Venus-rings round her neck and the larynx is delicately depicted. Hair and mural crown have been covered with gold leaf.

The goddess with the mural crown has been identified as the Tyche of Kalydon, but with a presumed tympanon and the find of a lion in the same room, the iconography points towards to the Anatolic goddess Cybele.

I.M. & S.D.

Pentelic marble. The sculpture is completely preserved except for small fragments from around the mane. The lion was painted and traces of red paint have been found on the pedestal. The lion rests on his back paws with upright front legs. The paws on the front and back legs are long with distinctive claws. The eyes are wide open and deeply set in the broad face which is surrounded by the mane. The nose is squarish with a smaller lower jaw, the mouth is open so that the canine teeth are visible. The mane runs down the middle of the neck in big volumous ringlets that become gradually shorter.

I.M. & S.D.

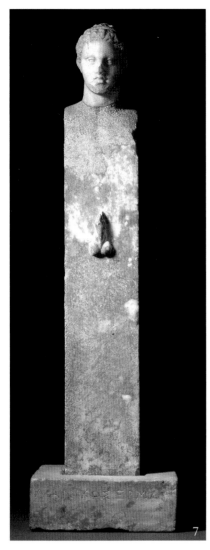

tip of the nose is broken off and missing and a fragments are missing from the left side of the chin. Finally, both wings have been broken off at the shaft. On the surface of the herma a thick and very hard layer of mixed earth and lime has formed an almost concrete-like mass. Only the most important areas on the herma have been cleaned such as the inscription, the face and the area around the erected penis. On the limestone base the dedication says: ΛΑΝΙΚΟΣ: ΕΡΜΑ

Lanikos is depicted as a young man with short curly hair wearing a round tiara (diadema) on his head. The shape of his face is oblong and rather chubby with a firm chin. The eyes are small with heavy eyelids and the small ears are simply flat without plasticity. The mouth has the shape of a rosebud, with full lips and is slightly open (an athlete).

I.M., S.D. & J.J.

7. Lanikos' herma
Agrinion Inv. no. 342,
Exc. no. F03-2424/2432
2nd cent. BC.
H 85 cm, of which the head and neck measure 22 cm, the shaft 55 cm and the base 8 cm.

The base is made of a hard bluish limestone while the herma is made of Pentelic marble. The herma is well preserved except for small fragments at a fracture on the neck. The

8. Lamp
Exc. no. F03-2177
Hellenistic type.
H 2.5 cm.

Wheel-made lamp with depressed disc foot. Tripartite loop handle.

9. Lamp
Exc. no. F03-2193
Hellenistic type.
H 2.0 cm.

Wheel-made lamp. Flat base and in-turned rim. Ring handle.

10. Lamp
Exc. no. F03-2426
Late 1st cent. BC to 1st cent. AD.
H 2.5 cm.

Moulded lamp with flat base and sunken discus. Edge of central filling hole preserved. Air hole near the flat topped nozzle. Designs on nozzle with volute on each side at junction to body. Moulded depiction of Heracles in centre.

I.M. & S.D.

11. Exaleiptron or clay lantern
Exc. no. F03-2360
Late 1st cent. BC to 1st cent. AD
H 12.8 cm.

Cylindrical bowl with circular stem. Restored from many fragments.

I.M. & S.D.

12. Antefix
Exc. no. F04-2127
3rd cent. BC.
H 27.5 cm.

Well preserved moulded antefix with lotus design
(11 leaves) above slanting palmettes.

I.M. & S.D.

13. Ridge tile
Exc. no. F04-2045
4th cent. BC.
H 17.5 cm.

Two faced palmette on a flat surface. Palmettes preserved with brown paint in between. They radiate
from a central core above spirals. Rosettes are seen
under the lower palmette petals.

I.M. & S.D.

16. Sima
Exc. no. F03-5023
Late 5th cent. BC.
L 16.4 cm.

Finely painted sima with red/brown and
black background paint and patterns in white
paint. Meander on bottom part. Bead and
reel, lotus and palmette motifs in the main
zone.

I.M. & S.D.

14. Antefix
Exc. no. F02-2027
Late 6$^{th}$ to early 5$^{th}$ cent. BC. Archaic.
H 10.5 cm.

Flat faced antefix with painted palmette, red and brown/blue petals framed by white. Scalloped edges.

I.M. & S.D.

15. Sima
Exc. no. F03-1035
Late 6$^{th}$ to early 5$^{th}$ cent. BC. Archaic.
H 12.5 cm.

Upper part only. Fragments of red painted palmette below red brown lotus petals. The rim is decorated with alternating brown and clay coloured rectangles.

I.M. & S.D.

17. Sime
Exc. no. F03-5024
5$^{th}$ cent. BC.
L 21.7 cm.

Sime with reddish brown band with main freeze white on dark base. Beda and reel. Two hanging palmettes and lotus pattern with white out-turning (11 petals) leaves. The lower side has a meander pattern.

I.M. & S.D.

# Zea Harbour Project

18

19

20

**18. Pan-tile**
Reg. no. L72.01 and L72.02
Piraeus mus.no. 10.550
5-4<sup>th</sup> cent. BC.
L 37.6 cm, W 29.9 cm, Th. 4.71 cm.

Corinthian type pan-tile collated from two fragments. Part of the lower narrow and left long side preserved. Lightbrown clay with inclusions. Thickness is reduced at the lower part. At the lower side and lengthwise of the narrow edge there is a cutting 5,1m wide. The left side is occupied by a low raised border. The lower surface is unpainted and rough while the upper and side surfaces are smooth and covered by light yellow slip which is transformed to light-whitish at the point where the cover tile was met.

**M.G.**

**19. Pan-tile**
Reg. no S32.03.1
5-4<sup>th</sup> cent. BC.
L 21.10 cm, W 16.80 cm, Th. 2.74-6.59 cm.

Fragment of Corinthian pan-tile with parts of two sides preserved. Pale yellow clay. The tile has two raised borders: the upper border and the right border. The upper border is *c.* 2.30 cm wide and raised *c.* 0.20 cm above the tile surface; the right border gradually merges with the upper border.

**M.S.**

21

**20. Cover-tile**
Reg no. L74.01
Pireaus mus.no. 10.551
5-4<sup>th</sup> cent. BC.
L 9.2 cm, W 8.7 cm, H 4.2 cm.

Fragment of Corinthian type cover-tile. Part of the top preserved. Light brown clay with inclusions. Triangular in shape with curved lower side. At the upper surface has light whitish slip.

**M.G.**

**21. Cover-tile**
Reg. no. S216.01.1
5-4<sup>th</sup> cent. BC.
L 5.80 cm, W 8.60 cm, H 1.50-3.50 cm.

Fragment of Corinthian gable-shaped cover-tile. Orange brown clay. The top of the gable is preserved but none of the bottom edges. The underside is curved. The top surface has remains of a thin pale yellow slip.

**M.S.**

48

# Roof construction

The shipshed complex at Zea harbour was one of the largest roof-covered building complexes of the Classical Period; at least one, but possibly several building phases were covered using a Corinthian tile roof, supported on limestone columns.

Superstructures covered by Corinthian pan- and cover-tiles always sloped in at least one direction. The alternating shorter/longer spacing between the colonnades in the upper (preserved) half of the shipshed complex suggests a saddle-roof design, i.e. sloping on two sides. The shipsheds were also built inclined towards the sea. Thus the roof sloped in three directions, which demanded a special placing of the tiles: the width of the pan-tile (L71.01 and L71.02) tapers towards the lower side, this implies that the roof tiles were placed so that the exposed leading edge of the tiles remained vertical to allow efficient rainwater run-off. Consequently the pan-tiles along the ridge and eaves (as with L71.01 and L71.02) needed to be trapezoidal so as to fit the unusual roof design. During the land excavations carried out in 2002 a pit was found containing a tile deposit and two fragments of kanta-haroi (L69.01 and L68.01). The rim fragment (L68.01) proves import-ant, providing evidence of the rebuilding of the shipsheds in the third quarter of the 4th century BC.

M.S.

22

23

22. Fish-plate
Reg no. L56.01
Pireaus mus.no. 10.552
First quarter of 3rd cent. BC.
Max. H 2.4 cm, Max. dim. 7.2 x 6,2 cm.

Part of the base and body from a black glazed fish-plate. Orange clay. Part of the base and body preserved. Chipped over the entire surface. Medallion shape base with curved outline, shallow body with slight curved walls. The beginning of the curving of the bottom is visible. Black, smooth glaze. Two bands, one in the transition from the base to the body and one around the bottom.

M.G.

23. Kantharos
Reg. no. L68.01
Pireaus mus.no.10.553
Third quarter of 4th cent. BC.
H 3.3 cm, W 5.9 cm.

Rim-fragment of black-glazed kan-tharos. Light brown clay. Small sec-tion of the neck and rim is preserv-ed. Chips and scraps in sections missing. Neck slightly curved. Lip manufactured in a mould, vertical with slightly concave outline, pro-truding. Black-brown glaze not equally fired.

M.G.

24. Kantharos
Reg. no. L69.01
Pireaus mus.no.10.554
6-5th cent. BC.
H 4.80 cm, W 5.80 cm, H of letters 0.9-1.6 cm.

Part of neck of black-glazed kan-tharos. Small chips and damaged in parts. Light orange clay. The neck slightly curved. Black, smooth glaze. Incised with letters after fir-ing. Four letters are distinguished: YPT and A or Δ.

M.G.

24

26

27

28

25

25. Transport amphora
Reg. no. S41.03
4th-2nd cent. BC?
L 17.1 cm, W 7.0 cm, Th.
2.1–3.6 cm.

Handle. Black clay. The handle attachment from the lower end is preserved. Remains of a thin matt brown slip on the external surface.

M.S.

26. Transport amphora
Reg. no. L61.01
Pireaus mus.no. 10.555
4th cent. BC.
H 11.8 cm, D of base 6.2 cm.

Toe of a Thassian type transport amphora. Reddish clay with inclusions. Part of the base and the lower part of the stem missing. Base curved in outline. The stem is solid, cylindrical elongated with slightly curved walls. The base is distinguished from the stem with a slight groove.

M.G.

27. Transport amphora
Reg. no. S25.03
4th cent. BC.
H 9.3 cm, W 9.0 cm, Th. 1.0- 2.5 cm, D c. 8.0 cm.

Rim fragment of a transport amphora. Dark grey clay. The lip is triangular, with an offset ridge just below. The neck slopes outwards. The amphora has remains of a thin matt pale yellow slip on the external surface.

M.S.

28. Transport amphora
Reg. no. S225.03.2
4th-2nd cent. BC?
L 7.80 cm, W 10.70 cm,
Th. 0.60–0.90 cm.

Body fragment of a transport amphora with remains of tar on the internal surface. Light brown orange clay. Remains of a yellow/brown slip on external surface.

M.S.

# Khania, Crete

## 29. Small jug
GSE 80-P 0112,
Khania mus.no. 5785
EM II (*c.* 2400 BC.)
H 13 cm, D of base 5.5 cm.

Completely preserved; restored. Light brown clay. Plain ware. Beak-spouted with a vertical, roll handle, a globular body and flat base. Hand-made. *AAA* 16 (1983), 6, fig. 3.

K.T.

## 30. Deep cup
GSE 89-P 0413
MM II (*c.* 1900-1700 BC.)
H 6,3 cm, D of base 4.3 cm.

Full profile preserved; a large part of the body and the handle is missing. Red, fine clay. White pale paint on dark red shiny slip. Semiglobular body, high, slightly flaring rim. Flat, slightly concave base that turns to a spiral relief inside. Two pairs of wavy bands run along the rim and the lower body; two more thin wavy bands are painted in between. Groups of five dots cover the space between the bands. Groups of vertical lines decorate the rim and the lower body. A cross pattern covers the exterior bottom of the base. The same pattern, but a larger one, decorates the interior of the base, encircled by dots. An example of protopalatial pottery from the settlement on the Kastelli hill. *AAA* 21 (1988), 20, fig. 6.

E.P.

## 31. Pyxis
GSE 73-P 0077,
Khania mus.no. 3620
End of LM IB (*c.* 1450 BC.)
H c. 11.7 cm, Int. D of rim 9.6 cm.

Completely preserved; restored. It was found on the floor of Room D of House I and is heavily burnt by the fire that destroyed the building complex. The cylindrical pyxis with the low collar neck, the horizontal shoulder, the small strap handles, set horizontally on the beginning of the body and the flat base is a characteristic fine ware example of the local LM IB pottery workshop. The light orange clay and the whitish, chalky wash on the exterior of the vase are typical characteristics, too. The decoration is restricted to groups of bands, except for a narrow zone on the upper body, which is covered by various iris and crocus flowers, a foliate band, running spirals and a net pattern. The painter follows, apparently, the conservative tradition of the so-called "sub-LM IA" or "abstract" or "standard tradition" ware. *AAA* 4 (1973), fig. 10.

M.A.-V.

**33. Bowl**
GSE 80-P 0864,
Khania mus.no. Π 5775
LM IIIB:1 (c. 1330–1250 BC.)
H 10 cm, D of rim 14.7 cm, D of
base 5 cm.

**34. Cup**
GSE 73-P 0765,
Khania mus.no. Π 3804
LM IIIB:1 (c. 1330–1250 BC.)
H 6.3 cm, D of rim 12.2 cm, D of
base 4.5 cm.

**32. Strainer**
GSE 84-P 3113,
Khania mus.no. 8394
End of LM IB (c. 1450 BC.)
H 16.7 cm, D of body 13.5 cm.

Completely preserved; restored. It was found in pieces on the floor of room C of House IV, burnt by the fire that destroyed the building complex. This strainer has the shape of the characteristic, local LM IB jug; a strained rim and a basket handle are the new features. The protrusions on the ends of the handle recall metallic prototypes. Both clay and wash are typical of the LM IB local workshop: reddish, gritty clay and whitish, chalky wash, restricted only to zones on the exterior. The decoration consists of bands in groups and a zone covered by a double, hatched zig-zag band set on upper body. It belongs to the "sub-LM IA" or "abstract" or "standard tradition" ware, as the previous example. *AAA* 18 (1985), 15, fig. 6.

M.A.-V.

Restored. Yellowish, fine clay. Brown-yellowish thick and shiny slip, that turns to grey at places. Brown to orange paint. Semiglobular body, straight rim, flat base. Two rounded horizontal handles. Bands run along the rim, the base and the top of the handles, while a wider one runs the body. The main decoration, between the handles, consists of a zone of alternating V pattern. Bands run the rim and the body while a spiral decorates the base internally. A product of the local Kydonian Workshop, the presence of which is quite intense during the 13th cent. B.C. The characteristic "personality" of the vases, with the fine clay and the yellowish shiny slip, makes the products of the workshop identifiable all over the Creto-Mycenaean world. *AAA* 16 (1983) 12, fig. 9.

E.P.

Large part of the body and the handle is restored. Cream-coloured, fine clay. Yellowish, thick and shiny slip. Black to brown paint. Semiglobular body, straight rim, flat base and a strap vertical handle. A wide band runs along the base and the perimeter of the bottom. A loop encircles the handle and ends to the rim band. A group of narrow bands runs along the body. The main decoration, between the bands, consists of groups of alternating arcs. A band runs along the rim and a spiral pattern along the base internally. Product of Kydonian Workshop.

E.P.

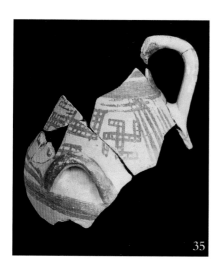

35

36

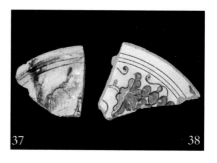

37 38

**35. Hydria**
GSE 71-P 0485
LG I (*c.* 750 BC.)
D of rim *c.* 11.8 cm.

Partly preserved; in sherds. It is a characteristic example of the local pottery workshop during the LG period, when the Khania settlement began to flourish again. Reddish brown, gritty clay. Flaring rim, biconical body, a vertical strap handle and two horizontal roll handles. Shoulder panel with groups of cross-hatched swastikas, in a "metopes and triglyphs" arrangement. The swastika was a common feature in Khania, during the Geometric times. *GSE* I (1997), 51-52, pl. 117.

M.A.-V.

**36. Amphora**
GSE 87-P 0077
Khania mus.no. 9493γ
1ˢᵗ quarter of 1ˢᵗ cent. BC.
Preserved H 32.5.

Upper body fragment: Neck, handles and part of rim. Clay light red, cream-coloured slip. Rectangular stamp ATTA on upper part of one handle. The other handle also carries a rectangular stamp but without letters. Similar stamp at the Athenian Agora. Italian type. *GSE* I, 204, 209 and pls. 64, 99:1a+b.

K.T.

**37. Painted Sgraffito bowl**
GSE 84-P 0099
15ᵗʰ-16ᵗʰ cent.
Max.pres.dim. 7 cm.

Rim and body fragment. Brown, hard clay. Double slip: light brown to greyish slip on both sides and white slip internal and over rim. Concentric sgraffito lines and loops enhanced with brown and green glaze. Analysed: local production. *GSE* I, 137, pls. 49, 78a:3, Frontispiece:f.

K.T.

**38. Painted, glazed plate**
GSE 80-P 0151
17ᵗʰ cent.
Max.pres.dim. 9.9 cm.

Body and base fragment. White hard and raw fabric (frit ware). Low ring base. Decoration of vines and grapes in blue and green with black outline. Late product of Iznik derivative ware. Analysed. Imitation Iznik. *GSE* I, 85, 174, pls. 90d:1, Frontispiece:a.

K.T.

41. *Nodulus*
GSE 76-TC 003,
Khania mus.no. Π 1561
End of LM IB (*c.* 1450 BC.)
L 2.4 cm, W 1.7 cm.

39. Linear A tablet
GSE 77-TC 133
Khania mus.no. KH 88
End of LM IB (*c.* 1450 BC.)
H 6 cm, W 4.6-4.8 cm, Th. 0.4-0.6 cm.

Partly preserved; burnt during the big conflagration of the building complex. Red, fine clay. Text in three lines. The first one consists of the syllabic signs AB 16-55-80 and AB 21f-118, which belong to two words. The second line begins with the ideogram AB 30 (for figs in Linear B), continues with the numeral 10 and ends with a word by the group of syllabograms AB 50-45 and a numeral. The numeral 8 possesses the third line. The inscription seems to be complete. It is obviously a list of quantities written in the Minoan script, still undeciphered. The tablet was found in House I, above the floor of the storeroom E. *SMEA* 19 (1977), 35-47; *GORILA* 5, 40-41.

M.A.-V.

40. Roundel
GSE 83-TC 005,
Khania mus.no. KH Wc 2118
End of LM IB (*c.* 1450 BC.)
D 5.4 cm, Th. 1.6 cm.

Almost completely preserved. Red clay with a few inclusions; burnt during the fire that destroyed the building complex. The ideogram AB 61 of the Linear A has been incised on the upper surface. Six identical impressions by the same seal on the periphery: two lions, sitting in opposite directions, a very common depiction in the roundels from Khania, executed in the "Cut Style". Fingerprints are visible on both sides. In the Minoan bureaucracy, the roundels were used as receipts. The greater amount of these objects belongs to Khania archives. This roundel was found in an LM IIIA:1 pit, which contained LM IB material as well. *Kadmos* 23 (1984), 8-9, pl. 2, Hallager 1996 II, 151; CMS V, Suppl.1A, no. 166.

M.A.-V.

Completely preserved. Reddish brown clay; burnt, during the fire that destroyed the building complex. Finger prints on its surface. On the obverse, an impression by an elliptical seal depicts the bull, the symbol of the Minoan power, in a flying gallop above a paved area. It is executed in the naturalistic way that characterizes the Neopalatial art and the scene probably hints to the bull leaping. The nodule, like the roundel, was not fastened to anything. It was probably used as a token or a docket. This nodule was found on the floor of Room D of House I, among other interesting items. CMS V Suppl. 1A, no. 145.

M.A.-V.

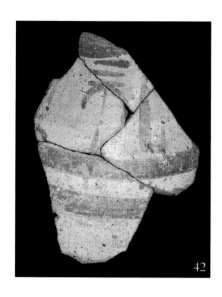

42

## 42. Stirrup jar
GSE 80-P 0858 (+80-P 0859),
Khania mus.no. KH Z 19
LM IIIB:1 (c. 1330-1250 BC.)
Max.pres.dim. 13 cm, Th. 0.9-1.2
cm.

Shoulder fragment of a stirrup jar
glued from four pieces. Clay
brown, semi-course, turning grey
towards inside. Light brown- whitish, dull slip. Light reddish-brown,
slightly shiny paint. The decoration
consists of a pair of bands around
the shoulder; traces of another one
band below the handle zone.
Between the bands, four Linear B
signs are preserved; the two ones in
the middle are identifiable with cer-
tainty: ]-na-ta-[. The inscription is
probably a male name. The same
inscription is also known from
Thebes. Product of the local
workshop. Kydonia appears to be
one of the main producers of in-
scribed stirrup jars. Vases full with
perfumed oil or wine were ex-
ported in the Mycenaean world.

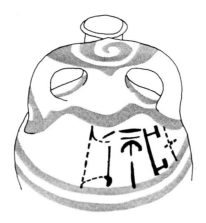

Inscription restored from the Khania
inscription and an inscription from
Thebes, ] ma-na-ta-ro[.

Examples of these vases have been
found in various palatial centers of
Mainland and Crete. *AAA* 16
(1983), 59-61, fig. 2.

E.P.

The complete inscription of the Khania
fragment as seen on one of the stirrup
jars from Thebes.

## 43. Stirrup jar
GSE 84-P 0204,
Khania mus.no. KH Z 39
LM IIIB:1/2 (c. 1300-1200 BC.)
MpH 7.5 cm, MpW 7.7 cm, Th.
0.8-0.9 cm.

Shoulder fragment of a stirrup jar.
Brown-red, semi-course, turning
grey towards inside clay. Reddish-
brown, slightly shiny paint. The
decoration consists of the remains
of two bands around the shoulder.
Between the bands remains of three
Linear B signs, one almost completely preserved: ] ta-*22-[de-so].
The same inscription is known
from one example from Khania and
five more from Thebes. The
inscription on all the vases above
was painted by the same hand.
Local workshop of Kydonia. *GSE*
III, 114, 214 and 274, pl. 114d:11.

E.P.

43

# Lone Simone Simonsen, tapestries

Lone Simone Simonsen graduated as a weaver and designer from The Danish Design School in Copenhagen in 1986 and has studied Modern Greek at universities in Sweden and Greece. Her works have been exhibited not only in Scandinavia, but also in Spain, Greece, Estonia, Latvia and Lithuania. She has recieved numerous awards and was granted scholarships to stay at the Danish Institute at Athens in 1994, 1995, 1996, 1997, and 1998.

Three *tapestries*. 60 x 60 cm.

Nine *Small works*, 40 x 40 cm. Here *Small work 5*.

# Per Weiss, pithos

In 1993 Per Weiss, Lene Regius, Bente Formann, Klavs Encke, and Kirsten Mus started The Pithoi Project in Thrapsano on Crete. Pithoi are large jars originally used for storage purposes. It was a workshop with Greeks and Danes following the old pottery traditions from the Minoan cultures of the second millennium BC. The clay was sourced locally. Greeks as well as Danes threw the material on the potter's wheel, the wares were fired in home-made kilns, the Danish ceramists then decorated them and fired them again. It was hard work! Many attempts were made, changes in the composure of the clay, adjustments of the kilns, but the final results were impressive; large beautifully shaped Greek pithoi dominated by Per Weiss's inspirations from Japan.

Per Weiss graduated from The Danish School of Art and Design in 1977 with supplementary studies in Japan. After his graduation he worked in Japan and had his own workshop there until 1985. When he returned to Denmark he established a number of workshops, his current being in 1988 with Lene Regius. His works have been presented on an individual basis as well as in group exhibitions in Scandinavia, Germany, Greece, Japan, and USA. He has received numerous awards and has exhibited his works at The Danish Institute at Athens in 1994.

Pithos, 1993.
H 97 cm.

# Karin Birgitte Lund, drawings

Karin Birgitte Lund has studied at The Royal Danish Academy of Arts from 1968-73. She has participated in exhibitions in Denmark, Sweden, Norway, Germany, India, and Taiwan. Her works are represented at museums in Scandinavia and New Delhi. She has received several scholarships and was granted a stay at The Danish Institute at Athens in 2005.

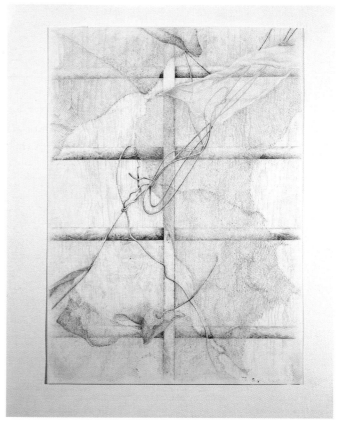

*Delfi* 1986. Tegning på papir. 86 x 68 cm.

*Arkaisk marmorhund* 2005. Tegning på lærred. 165 x 70 cm.

# Per-René Larsen, glass sculpture

As a means of expression hot glass has its limitations as well as unique possibilities. On one hand it contains such a big amount of charm, beauty and selling features. On the other hand the physical qualities of the material give exactly the resistance (the physical limitation and the process-dependant work) which becomes the dogma that gives the great freedom now that I have reached so far with my craftwork abilities. Exactly this ambiguity in the material makes the hot glass an important artistic media for me. As an artist I work with hot glass from an archaic sculptural point of view. But at the same time I am seeking to add the edge to the common that is able to create an importance beyond the aesthetics.

Per-René Larsen studied at the Copenhagen Arts and Craft School and at the Glass Academy in Orrefors, Sweden from 1972-76. He has participated in exhibitions in Scandinavia, Germany, Holland, England, Luxemburg, Belgium, Japan and USA. He has established the glass workshops Snoldelev Glasbrug Amba and Fanefjord Glas which he now runs as a craftsman-designer and artist. He has received several awards and has exhibited his works at the Danish Institute at Athens in 2003.

*Strange-angel*
Glass
c. 30 x 25 cm.

# Jytte Loehr, paintings

Jytte Loehr studied at The Academy of Fine Arts in Brussels, at studios in Copenhagen, Paris and Greece and at a workshop in Japan. She has exhibited every year since 1977 in Copenhagen and participated in individual as well as group exhibitions in Brussels, Paris, London, Athens, Rhodes, Vilnius and Rostock. She has received several scholarships and has stayed at The Danish Institute at Athens in 1996, 1999, 2002, and 2003.

*Himmelflugt*
130 x 97 cm.

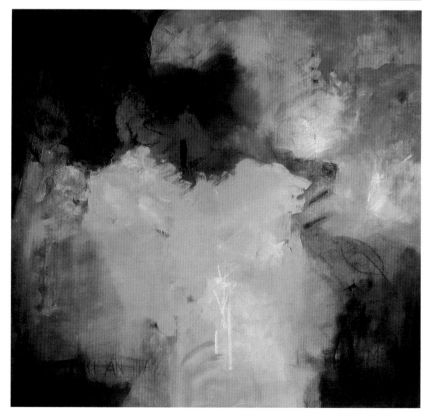

*Wherever you go,*
*a miracle awaits you,*
140 x 150 cm.

# Misja Rasmussen, bronze sculpture

This sculpture has been inspired by an inner power, strength. Also by a simplicity in the shape itself which I suppose is very Greek! I have chosen this sculpture because it is modern, but also very classic. Its modernity shows by the fact that it is a contemporary body and that its surface is fractured which gives it a mystical touch, an untold story we must find ourselves. Exactly like a geological find!

Misja Kristoffer Rasmussen has studied at The Academy of Arts in Milano and at the Art College Thorstedslund in Denmark. His works have been presented at numerous exhibitions at galleries and museums in Denmark, Italy, Ireland, and France. He has been the winner of international competitions and has received several scholarships. He was granted a stay at The Danish Institute at Athens in 2005.

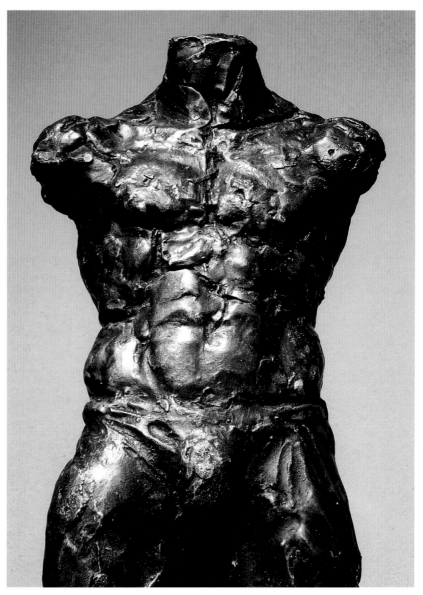

*The boxer – Ὁ πύκτης*
Bronze
45 x 15 x 12 cm.

# Nina Hole, ceramic sculpture

Nina Hole graduated from the Copenhagen Art and Craft School in 1963, from Glyptoteket's Art School in 1966 and has studied at colleges and ceramic workshops in New York. Her sculptures are exhibited all over the world. She participates in competitions and has won several awards. She is a frequent lecturer and takes part in workshops and symposia worldwide. She has received several scholarships, among these a stay at The Danish Institute at Athens in 1999.

The sculpture consists of inverted compound houses. Usually I draw inspiration from architecture. From the brand new modern buildings to the oldest ones from the earliest cultures with strong simple shapes along with rough surfaces and the range of colours which especially interest me. For this reason I burn my sculptures in a wood-fired kiln placing them in the firing flue so that they will be exposed to the greatest heat during three days of firing. In this way wear of time shows in the shape.

Wood-Fired Stoneware –
*Architectural forms.*
21 x 50 x 29 cm.

# Illustrations

Most illustrations in this book are from the photographic archive of the Danish Institute at Athens: pp. 9 (right), 12, 13 (left and right top) and 15-27.

From other schools and Institutions
Ny Carlsberg Glyptotek, p. 8 (left).
Kunstakademiet, p. 8 (right), 9 (centre).
Nationalmuseet, Copenhagen, p. 10 (left).
Ecole Française d'Athene: p. 14.

A few illustrations have been reproduced from publications:
A. Papanicolaou-Christensen, *Christian Hansen* (1994): p. 9 (left).
*Sfinx*, 1992, 1993, and 1999: pp. 10 (right), 11 (left), 13 (bottom right), and 28-29.
A. Evans, *Palace of Minos* I (1921): p. 11 (middle).
H. Boyd, *Gournia* (1908): p. 11 (right).

All illustrations from the archaeological projects are by the excavators or the projects:
Chalkis: pp. 30-31 and 42-43.
Kalydon: pp. 32-33, 44-47.
Zea Harbour: 34-35 (reconstruction drawings by Ioannis Nakas), pp. 48-50.
Mt. Pilion: p. 36.
Khania: pp. 38-39, 51-55.
Asklepeion: p. 40 (reconstruction Michalis Lefantis and Jesper Jensen).

All photographs of works of art and the artists (pp. 56-62) are on the responsibility of the artists except the pithos p. 57 and the sculpture p. 62 which are from the DIA archives.

# Bibliographic abbreviations used in catalogue

| | |
|---|---|
| *AAA* | *Athens Annals of Archaeology.* |
| *CMS* | Corpus der minoischen und mykenischen Siegel. |
| *GORILA* | *Recueil des inscriptions en Linéaire A,* 1-5 (Études Crétoises 21) Paris 1976-1985. |
| *GSE* | *The Greek-Swedish Excavations,* Stockholm 1997-. |
| Hallager 1996 | *The Minoan Roundel* (Aegaeum 14), Liége 1996. |
| *SMEA* | Studi Micenei ed Egeo Anatolici. |

# Selected bibliography

About the Institute

*Det Danske Institut i Athen. Beretning 1992-93*, Athen 1994 (by Søren Dietz).
*Det Danske Institut i Athen. Beretning 1994-95*, Athen 1996 (by Søren Dietz).
Web site: www.diathens.com

About the excavations

*Kephellenia*
Randsborg, K., *Kephallénia. Archaeology and history. The ancient Greek cities* I-II (Acta Archaeologica, Suppl. IV:1-2), København 2002.

*Rhodes*
Dietz. S. & E. Karanzali in *Sfinx* (1995), 36; and Lund J. in *Sfinx* (1999), 58.

*Chalkis*
Dietz. S., L. Kolonas, I. Moschos & S. Houby Nielsen, Preliminary reports in *Proceedings of the Danish Institute at Athens* II (1998), pp. 232-311; III (2000), 219-289; IV (2004) 167-227.
Dietz, S. & Y. Moschos (eds.), *Chalkis, Aitolias. The Prehistoric periods* (Monographs of the Danish Institute at Athens vol. 7), Athens 2006.

*Kalydon*
Dietz, S., 'En helligdom for Kalydons bygudinde', *Carlsbergondets Årsskrift* 2005, 148-63.
Dietz, S. & I Moschos, 'Kalydon en udgravning i Vestgrækenland', *Danske Museer* 6 (2005).
Preliminary report in *Proceedings of the Danish Institute at Athens* V (forthcoming).
Web site: www.kalydon.net

*Zea Harbour*
Blackman, D. "The shipsheds" in *Greek oared ships 900-322 BC.*, J.S. Morrison & R.T. Williams (eds), Cambridge 1968, 181-192.
Lovén, B., 'Flådestation Zea' *Sfinx* (2004), 149-154.
Web site: www.zeaharbourproject.dk

*Khania*
Hallager, E., *The Master Impression* (SIMA vol. 69), Göteborg 1985.
Hallager, E, & B.P. Hallager (eds.), *The Greek-Swedish Excavations at the Agia Aikaterini Square Kastelli, Khania 1070-1987.*
I.1-2. *From the Geometric to the Modern Greek Period*, Stockholm 1997.
II. *The Late Minoan IIIC settlement*, Stockholm 2000.
III.1-2. *The Late Minoan IIIB:2 settlement*, Stockholm 2003.